Simply Napoleon

Simply Napoleon

J. DAVID MARKHAM AND MATTHEW ZARZECZNY

SIMPLY CHARLY
NEW YORK

Cover Illustration by José Ramos
Cover Design by Scarlett Rugers

permissions@simplycharly.com

ISBN: 978-1-943657-19-3

Brought to you by http://simplycharly.com

To our mothers, with love,
Myrtle Sturgis Markham and Sharon Marie Zarzeczny

Contents

Praise for *Simply Napoleon*

"From being the *enfant terrible* of the Bonaparte clan, to his torrid letters to Josephine, to his conquest and reorganization of Europe, Napoleon Bonaparte is portrayed as both man of the flesh and man of destiny in *Simply Napoleon*. There is nothing simple about *Simply Napoleon*; it is a carefully researched, well-written, condensed version of the Napoleonic era. Here the reader will find the ogre and brigand (according to his detractors), masterful general, reforming emperor, imperial majesty, and ultimately prisoner. Napoleon was both despondent and jubilant, and readers of this book will find themselves in the same conundrum."

–Susan P. Conner, Professor of History Emerita and retired Provost, Albion College, Michigan

"What a little gem! If you are looking for a quick biography of Napoleon, look no further. With lively narrative and good mastery of facts, *Simply Napoleon* will take you on a thrilling journey recounting Napoleon's rise to power from his humble beginnings on the island of Corsica to the emperor of much of Europe. Highly recommended for those wanting a brief refresher on one of the greatest European statesmen. This is both an entertaining and an enlightening read!"

–Alexander Mikaberidze, Sybil T. and J. Frederick Patten Professor of History and Social Sciences at Louisiana State University in Shreveport

"Well-researched and plainly written, *Simply Napoleon* is a good, readily accessible introduction to Napoleon and his military leadership, providing essential geopolitical context and psychological motivations for his campaigns. For those interested in learning more, the authors provide an excellent list of suggested works."

–Wayne Hanley, author of *The Genesis of Napoleonic Propaganda, 1796-1799* and Professor of History at West Chester University

"On a subject as vast as Napoleon, perhaps the greatest challenge is not to include everything, but rather to cull the information down to a digestible form. In this, both authors have achieved the Herculean task of presenting the key information needed to begin to come to grips with perhaps the most influential and fascinating man in history. If you have not yet approached the history of Napoleon and his era, then run out and get this book so that you may begin to appreciate all that is offered."

–Todd Fisher, Executive Director of the Napoleonic Historical Society

"*Simply Napoleon* provides a clear, quick, and readable work that can be absorbed by anyone desiring a brief look at Napoleon Bonaparte's life and accomplishments. The annotated suggested reading list provides the tools necessary for readers who are intrigued and tantalized by this man to dig deeper into the great Napoleon's life and lasting legacy. *Simply Napoleon* provides an uncluttered starting point from which to embark upon an investigative journey into the life of this very complicated man."

–George N. Vourlojianis, Professor Emeritus of History at John Carroll University

"If I were to recommend a book on Napoleon that would turn mild interest into full-blown obsession, *Simply Napoleon* would be among my top two choices. The authors' ability to weave such a comprehensive narrative of the most salient facts without losing some of the details in the grand story of Napoleon is unparalleled. In style, both academics and casual readers will enjoy the almost conversational approach to the history of the Napoleonic Era. This book is a must-have for both nascent and well established Napoleonic libraries."

–Kevin F. Rodriguez, Fellow of the International Napoleonic Society, Social Media Director, Napoleonic Historical Society

"An enjoyable read, *Simply Napoleon* serves as an excellent introduction to Napoleon Bonaparte, his times, and his legacy. While written for those new to Napoleon and Napoleonic history, *Simply Napoleon* will also prove useful to scholars with its enlightening anecdotes that illustrate the views of Napoleon and his contemporaries. Even those familiar with Napoleonic history are likely to discover new information while reading *Simply Napoleon*. Recommended for both newcomers and experts alike."

–Nathan D. Jensen, Fellow of the International Napoleonic Society, owner/writer of www.frenchempire.net

"If you have ever wondered why Napoleon inspires interest not just in France but around the world even to this day, *Simply Napoleon* provides the quick and easy introduction regardless of background. This blitz through the storied life of the man himself nevertheless still finds time to connect larger international currents from the Society of United Irishmen to the Haitian Revolution. While the authors admire Napoleon, their subject remains human, and great efforts are made to present a rounded figure for the reader to judge, including a useful annotated guide for further reading. However one views the French general and emperor, the book's central point is achieved with abundant clarity: an understanding of the modern world is incomplete without Napoleon."

–Nicholas Stark, Adjunct Instructor of History at Union County College

"Packed with facts and interwoven with extensive excerpts from

Napoleon's correspondence and speeches, this is a popular yet painstaking biography that does not take sides or grind critical axes. Instead, it aims to provide interested readers with an entertaining and sympathetic portrait of one of history's most astonishing leaders. The authors are noted experts on their subject, providing sure guidance through the thicket of facts, theories, and speculation that surrounds Bonaparte and ably curating additional research for readers who are enticed to learn more."

–Yvonne Bruce, Lecturer in English at John Carroll University

Other *Great Lives*

Simply Austen by Joan Klingel Ray
Simply Beckett by Katherine Weiss
Simply Beethoven by Leon Plantinga
Simply Chekhov by Carol Apollonio
Simply Chomsky by Raphael Salkie
Simply Chopin by William Smialek
Simply Darwin by Michael Ruse
Simply Descartes by Kurt Smith
Simply Dickens by Paul Schlicke
Simply Dirac by Helge Kragh
Simply Einstein by Jimena Canales
Simply Eliot by Joseph Maddrey
Simply Euler by Robert E. Bradley
Simply Faulkner by Philip Weinstein
Simply Fitzgerald by Kim Moreland
Simply Freud by Stephen Frosh
Simply Gödel by Richard Tieszen
Simply Hegel by Robert L. Wicks
Simply Hitchcock by David Sterritt
Simply Joyce by Margot Norris
Simply Machiavelli by Robert Fredona
Simply Nietzsche by Peter Kail
Simply Proust by Jack Jordan
Simply Riemann by Jeremy Gray
Simply Sartre by David Detmer
Simply Tolstoy by Donna Tussing Orwin
Simply Stravinsky by Pieter van den Toorn
Simply Turing by Michael Olinick
Simply Wagner by Thomas S. Grey
Simply Wittgenstein by James C. Klagge

Series Editor's Foreword

Simply Charly's "Great Lives" series offers brief but authoritative introductions to the world's most influential people—scientists, artists, writers, economists, and other historical figures whose contributions have had a meaningful and enduring impact on our society.

Each book provides an illuminating look at the works, ideas, personal lives, and the legacies these individuals left behind, also shedding light on the thought processes, specific events, and experiences that led these remarkable people to their groundbreaking discoveries or other achievements. Additionally, every volume explores various challenges they had to face and overcome to make history in their respective fields, as well as the little-known character traits, quirks, strengths, and frailties, myths, and controversies that sometimes surrounded these personalities.

Our authors are prominent scholars and other top experts who have dedicated their careers to exploring each facet of their subjects' work and personal lives.

Unlike many other works that are merely descriptions of the major milestones in a person's life, the "Great Lives" series goes above and beyond the standard format and content. It brings substance, depth, and clarity to the sometimes-complex lives and works of history's most powerful and influential people.

We hope that by exploring this series, readers will not only gain new knowledge and understanding of what drove these geniuses, but also find inspiration for their own lives. Isn't this what a great book is supposed to do?

Charles Carlini, Simply Charly
New York City

Preface

"Napoleon is the greatest man that has ever lived ... Since the world has existed there has never appeared a general, a conqueror, or a king, who can be compared to him." With these words, Louis Bonaparte, a relatively short-reigning ruler of Holland in the early 19th century, lauded his more illustrious brother. While this praise may seem like a fraternal hyperbole, Louis was hardly alone in this grandiose assessment, although we disagree that Napoleon cannot be compared to anyone else in history. Still, we, like many historians before us, would only offer a handful of names for such a comparison.

Napoleon Bonaparte, or Emperor Napoleon I, was without any doubt one of the most influential and remarkable people who has ever lived. Only an elite group of individuals are reasonably categorized in the same class as Napoleon: Alexander the Great, Julius Caesar, and Charlemagne—all of whom Napoleon admired and compared himself to—can justifiably be placed alongside Napoleon as the truly "greatest men" of human history. The importance of these leaders as military innovators, empire builders, and so much more is difficult to quantify.

To that end, *Simply Napoleon* should bring a well-researched look at France's legendary emperor and military commander to a wide general audience, including those who have heard of Napoleon (yes, there is even a Pizza Hut commercial in which the current United States President Donald Trump compares himself to Napoleon) and yet do not really know the history of this iconic figure. This book is written in an easily readable manner without the technical jargon often found in biographies and studies directed at a primarily academic audience of our fellow professors. Moreover, it is intended as a fairly concise overview of Napoleon's life and times, and serves as a sort of introduction and study guide of the great man and his many groundbreaking accomplishments.

Although he is the central figure of this volume, Napoleon is joined by a veritable cast of fascinating people who played their own roles in influencing Bonaparte's life, as well as his successes and failures. In the coming pages, you will learn about Napoleon's tumultuous love life (he was married twice and had many mistresses), as well as his large family with ambitious brothers and sisters who would join Napoleon in ruling various kingdoms and principalities in Europe. Napoleon also had to contend with members of Europe's traditional ruling dynasties—the Bourbons, Habsburgs, Hohenzollerns, and Romanovs, who were sometimes allied with the Bonapartes and at other times, their bitter enemies. The story of Napoleon goes beyond the lives of monarchs and their spouses to include diplomats, lawyers, politicians, priests, rebels, scientists, and soldiers—all of whom had in some way shaped the emperor's private, public, and military life. Statesmen helped negotiate the treaties that redrew the world's maps. Lawyers and politicians enacted laws under Napoleon's guidance that would be adapted by countries across the world from Asia to North America. Bishops, priests, and even rabbis all worked with Napoleon in the undertaking of numerous religious reforms, including a Concordat between Napoleonic France and the Holy See that lasted for over 100 years, from 1801 to 1905, foreshadowing agreements made between Fascist Italy (in 1929) and Nazi Germany (in 1933) with the Holy See in the 20th century. Thus, because the Napoleonic Code, the French civil code established in 1804, and the Concordat of 1801 are accepted as two of the most important and influential documents in all of modern world history, their authors are worthy of remembering. So too are the rebels in Haiti and Spain who unleashed horrors on Napoleon's forces; while we do address these atrocities, we only scratch the surface of the darkest moments of the era. Far less disturbing were the architects, artists, scholars, and scientists of that era. Working on Napoleon's behalf, they advanced our understanding of Ancient Egypt, while also producing some of the finest paintings and monuments that are still visited and admired every day by millions of people from around the world.

Finally, we also mention the many soldiers who fought, bled, and in many cases even died, in the numerous battles and campaigns fought by Napoleon and his subordinates in battlefields around the world.

This book will enlighten our readers about the life of a military genius who led armies to Egypt, the Holy Land, and across Europe. Napoleon sent his forces to battle Haitians in the Caribbean and doubled the size of the United States with one of history's most celebrated real estate deals–the Louisiana Purchase. But he was more than just a conqueror and gifted general. He was also an activist of sorts, bringing reforms to France's education and legal system, the positive changes that far outlasted Napoleon's conquests and influenced–in some cases to this day–reforms in many other countries as well. Having achieved so much in one of history's most turbulent eras, that of the French Revolution, Napoleon has been the subject of countless works of art, literature, and cinema. Everything from restaurants (Napoleon's Pizza) to psychological conditions (Napoleon complex) have been named after him. Once again, few men or women have had such an enduring influence on the world's military, education systems, laws, and popular culture.

His accomplishments during his life were significant, and so too were his failures. Not everyone who acknowledges Napoleon as an important or influential figure necessarily sees him as a "great" man in a positive sense. Both during and after his life, he has had his share of venomous detractors who pointed to the death toll of his many wars as his truest legacy. Although such luminous men as Britain's erstwhile Prime Minister Winston Churchill disagreed with comparisons of Napoleon with Adolf Hitler, others, including our fellow contemporary historian Claude Ribbe, embrace parallels between the French emperor and the German dictator. In his 2005 book *Le Crime de Napoleon* (Napoleon's Crime), Ribbe alleged that Napoleon's forces used Sulphur Dioxide gas to mass execute over 100,000 rebellious blacks on Saint-Domingue (now Haiti) and Guadeloupe, an action that Ribbe saw as a model for Hitler's

Holocaust in the 20th century. Ribbe is hardly the only scholar to present Napoleon in such a negative light. American historian Alan Schom wrote a lengthy and maligned biography of Napoleon published in 1997 that is anything but flattering. In a review of this book on the website The Napoleon Series (https://www.napoleon-series.org), Kevin Kiley, author of the much more positively reviewed *Artillery of the Napoleonic Wars* (2004), denounced Schom for, among other things, doing "his prejudiced best to blacken Napoleon's reputation." Ribbe and Schom may represent some of the most notable recent historians to criticize Napoleon sharply, but they are preceded by numerous people of diverse backgrounds from as far back as Napoleon's life. To see negative perceptions of Bonaparte dating back to his lifetime, one need only look at the many cartoons by such artists as Britain's James Gillray that present mocking caricatures of Napoleon akin to what we see in newspapers today of our present politicians. Over the course of Napoleon's career and after, cartoonists, pamphleteers, and some of Europe's propagandists continued to ridicule Napoleon and even portray him as an antichrist. As you will learn in the following pages, alongside the positive descriptions of Bonaparte as a hero and humanitarian, a number of his contemporaries and some modern scholars have denounced him as "bad" and even "evil."

How can one and the same person be revered as "the greatest man who ever lived" by some, and denounced as a warmongering and even genocidal tyrant by others? Why has he been so polarizing and controversial? Or was Napoleon, as we would argue, more complicated than to be classified as either "good" or "evil?" Is he as British historian David Chandler asserted "a great bad man" or is another description more accurate? By reading this volume, you will perhaps develop your own opinion of this much-debated and perhaps even misunderstood man.

In the pages that follow, we seek to explore many facets of Napoleon and his policies in chapters organized chronologically by key phases of his life. We start with his childhood, which had an unquestionable formative influence upon him, especially his upbringing by his mother, and then explore his education and early military schooling before moving on to his career as an officer in the French army amid the tumult of the French Revolution. From there, we see how Napoleon rose through the ranks to lead French forces in their conquests of Italy and then Egypt in a manner sometimes compared (even by Napoleon himself) to the exploits of Alexander the Great. Our next chapter sees Napoleon lead France as a reform-minded "Consul" reminiscent of the flurry of activity undertaken by ancient Roman Consul and Dictator Julius Caesar nearly two millennia earlier. Afterward, Napoleon traded the trappings of republicanism for something more akin to establishing a Charlemagne-esque imperial system that dominated Western Europe. Afterward, we focus first on the period of imperial glory, followed by Napoleon's precipitous fall and eventual final defeat. We continue with his life and death in exile before concluding with an examination of the aftermath—Napoleon's legacy that endures to the present, as is evident by even your reading this volume today.

Our coverage within these ten chapters includes some topics that go beyond just a narrative of Napoleon's life to place him in his historical context and to show how extensive his influence was on world history. As you can tell already from the preceding paragraphs, his significance was and still is widespread. Indeed, modern historians from Paul Fregosi to J. P. Riley have written books with titles that explicitly refer to the Napoleonic Wars as a "world war." Yet, as we mentioned above, Bonaparte was more than merely a military figure. His varied accomplishments have helped shape the world we live in today and, for better or worse, without Napoleon's influence on so many aspects of our history, the world today would likely be a quite different place. It is hardly surprising then that numerous articles, essays, and books addressing various counterfactuals or "what ifs" of the Napoleonic Age continue to speculate how even seemingly minor changes in Napoleon's life could have had far-reaching consequences. We continue to ask questions and search for answers about this beguiling man who has arguably influenced all of us in a variety of ways. Was he really the greatest man who ever lived? Read on and reach your own conclusion!

As for Napoleon, his journey (well, as is the case with all of us, really) began when he first entered our world. Nearly 10 years before the birth of Louis Bonaparte and many decades before Louis's designation of his older brother as history's greatest man, the birth of Napoleon Bonaparte to his mother, Letizia, would commence a life only paralleled by a handful of individuals. So, let us start with the story of a boy and his mother, and how this relationship changed the course of world history.

J. David Markham
Toronto, ON

Matthew Zarzeczny
Ashland, OH

Acknowledgements

To acknowledge all those who have helped David in his career would take an entire book! Napoleonic history luminaries like Don Horward, Jerry Gallaher, Rafe Blaufarb, and others certainly have made a huge difference. Other friends in the International Napoleonic Society, the Napoleonic Historical Society, the Consortium on the Revolutionary Era, and the Massena Society have always been there to offer support and help. The late Proctor Patterson Jones and, of course, his friend and the founder of the INS, the late Ben Weider, were very important in his development. He is also grateful for his friend Matthew's willingness to join in this project.

Closer to home, David's parents always encouraged his interests, though when his dad, James, introduced him to Napoleon, no one probably suspected where that would lead! David's sister, Sara, her husband, Ron, and their son, Adam, have always been supportive as well, even if they are not Napoleon's biggest fans. David's ex-wife and now close friend, Barbara Munson, was instrumental in his success for many years, serving as his editor for all of his books and articles. And finally, he wants to give special tribute to his wife, Edna. Her support in the past few years has motivated him to continue moving forward. But then again, Edna's ancestors were from Prussia, home of Marshal Blücher, a.k.a. "Marshal Forwards!"

In addition to Matthew's parents, Daniel and Sharon Zarzeczny, brother- and sister-in-law David and Regina Zarzeczny (as well as his niece and nephews Alexis, Elias, and James), and miniature dachshund (appropriately named Marie Louise Zarzeczny), Matthew would like to thank Dr. David Foster at Ashland University; Drs. Matthew Berg, Yvonne Bruce, Rodney Hessinger, Daniel Kilbride, Anne Kugler, Maria Marsilli, and George Vourlojianis at John Carroll University; Drs. Leslie Heaphy, Ralph Menning, James Seelye, Shawn Selby, Thomas Sosnowski, and Lindsay Starkey as well as adjuncts

Christine Bowman and Angela Saunders at Kent State University at Stark; and Drs. Alice Conklin, Nathan Rosenstein, Richard Ugland, and Dale Van Kley at The Ohio State University, as well as Shell Harris at TopTenz.net and Beth Murina Michaels of Unique Interpretations, for their continued support and encouragement in his academic and professional careers. Matthew also wishes to thank his many students for their enthusiasm and diligence, which makes sharing his love of history that much more rewarding an experience. To that end, he especially recognizes the inspiring achievements of his students Eugene Claridge, Bryan Mersol, and Amber Hanophy, who have excelled both in and outside of the classroom. Lastly, Matthew wishes to recognize the many members of John Carroll University's Paranormal Research Group, the award-winning student organization that he advises, for making his academic career that much more unique and interesting.

Thank you from both of us to our editors, Helena Bachmann and John Meyer, for their careful examination of our manuscript. We greatly appreciate their hard work in helping us produce a more smoothly worded contribution to the *Simply Charly* series. Finally, we must also thank Charles Carlini for the opportunity to participate in this wonderful series of biographies.

Nearly all images used in this book, excluding the cover and a few images in the Public Domain reproduced here from *Wikipedia*, are from the David Markham Collection.

1. The Little Corsican: Napoleon's Childhood (1769-1789)

As a youth growing up on his island home of Corsica, the future emperor of the French and one of history's greatest conquerors, Napoleon Bonaparte, already wore a military uniform. On a particularly painful occasion, the young Napoleon's mother, Letizia, dealt him a sharp punishment. She tricked her son into believing that he had been invited to dine by the island's governor. Then, as Napoleon changed his clothes, she seized him, laid him across her knee, and proceeded to spank him. Why? He and his sister, Pauline had earlier mocked their hobbling grandmother, Letizia's mother. Whereas her mother spanked Pauline immediately when Letizia learned of her children's misbehavior, Napoleon could not justly be punished while wearing his sacred uniform.

This incident says much about Napoleon's upbringing. Although his mother was not formally educated, she demonstrated practical intelligence throughout her life. She also had an undeniable sense of dignity, frugality, and tenacity, as might be expected of a woman who had endured some of the later months of her pregnancy with Napoleon while a refugee in the mountains of Corsica. Ever since his birth, on Aug. 15, 1769, his mother instilled a strong sense of stern discipline in young Napoleon, befitting a descendant of minor nobility.

An engraving of Napoleon's mother, Leticia Bonaparte.

Letizia was born in 1750 in Ajaccio, Corsica, then part of the Republic of Genoa. Her father was a captain of Corsican

Regiments of Chivalry and Infantry in the Genoese army. After he died, her mother married a Swiss-born captain in the service of Genoa who was stationed on Corsica. In 1764, when just a teenager, Letizia married a Corsican lawyer, Carlo Buonaparte, who was five years her senior. Carlo would become Napoleon's father. Yet the job of raising the sometimes-rambunctious future emperor mostly fell to his mother. Near the end of his life, Napoleon reflected from his exile on St. Helena, "I was very well brought up by my mother. I owe her a great deal. She instilled into me pride and taught me good sense." That is not to say Napoleon always went along with his mother's wishes. As the award-winning author Elaine Landau recounted, "Sometimes he traded the loaf of fine white bread his mother gave him to take to school for a piece of the soldiers' tough dark bread. Napoleon claimed he didn't want to be pampered and preferred to eat like a real soldier." Nevertheless, Letizia made a sound effort to be something of a maternal general to her little soldier. Landau explained that when "she found out that Napoleon had been less than truthful, she whipped him soundly. Letizia could be harsh, but she instilled a desire in Napoleon to do well and complete any task he undertook. Throughout Napoleon's childhood, Letizia served as the disciplinarian . . . ."

Napoleon's father, Charles Bonaparte reproduced here from Wikipedia.

While reining in the notoriously ambitious Napoleon was an impressive enough feat, Madame Buonaparte did so while raising seven other children who survived infancy. She bore 13 children altogether, but five died as infants. In addition to Napoleon and

Pauline, the siblings included Joseph, born in 1768; Lucien, born in 1775; Elisa, born in 1777; Louis, born in 1778; Caroline, born in 1782, and Jérôme, born in 1784. All seven of Napoleon's brothers and sisters who lived to adulthood would eventually hold a royal or imperial title. From 1804 to 1814 and again in 1815, Napoleon held the most prestigious title, emperor of the French. Joseph held the next most prestigious title, reigning as king of Spain from 1808 to 1813. Lucien, although the third oldest of Letizia's children to survive infancy, received his imperial title last due to a falling out with his older brother Napoleon. Lucien reigned as prince of Canino from 1814 to 1840. Napoleon's youngest brothers joined Joseph in ruling kingdoms in their own rights. Louis reigned as king of Holland from 1806 to 1810, and Jérôme reigned as king of Westphalia from 1807 to 1813. As for Napoleon's sisters, Elisa reigned as grand duchess of Tuscany from 1809 to 1814, the beautiful Pauline served as Duchess of Guastalla in 1806, and the ambitious Caroline was queen consort of Naples from 1808 to 1815. All eight of the Bonaparte children owed much of their development to their mother. Indeed, as Letizia once acknowledged, "No one in the world has spanked so many kings and queens as I have."

While Napoleon's mother raised him, his father ascended a ladder of noble titles. Carlo's first notable appointment, in 1769, was as assessor of the royal jurisdiction of Ajaccio and the neighboring districts. That same year, he became a doctor in law at the University of Pisa, and before the year was up, he also became an advocate of the Superior Council of Corsica. He continued his ascent in 1770 when he was named substitute procurator of the king of France in Ajaccio. The following year, he became the assessor of the royal jurisdiction of Ajaccio and deputy of the nobility in the General States of Corsica. In 1772, he became a member of the Council of the Twelve Nobles of Dila, in western Corsica. In 1777, his newest title was Deputy of the Nobility of Corsica at the French royal court. Finally, in 1778, he was named Corsica's representative to the court of Louis XVI of France at Versailles. The continued successes of Carlo's career provided Napoleon with an example of what a brave man with common sense can accomplish.

While his mother influenced the first 10 years of Napoleon's childhood more directly than his father did, Carlo's political standing had a major effect on Napoleon's teenage years. In early 1779, not long after Carlo's appointment to represent Corsica at the French court, Napoleon was enrolled at a religious school in Autun, France. Both Napoleon and his elder brother Joseph attended this school. An interesting incident between the two boys in their early schooling foreshadowed their later relationship. In a mock combat, their schoolmaster pitted Joseph, representing the Romans, against Napoleon, who represented the Carthaginians. The younger brother protested being assigned the losing side until his more conciliatory sibling gave in and swapped sides. Whereas their father wanted Joseph to continue to receive religious instruction, Carlo set Napoleon on the path toward a military career. A few months after entering Autun, the nine-year-old Napoleon was admitted to a military academy at Brienne-le-Château.

The École Militaire de Brienne was prestigious and exclusive. To enroll Napoleon, Carlo had to prove that his family had been noble for at least four generations. Doing so meant delving into the family's long history. The family name goes back to the 1260s when William, a Florentine, took the surname now styled "Bonaparte," but then spelled "Buonaparte," meaning "good" (*buona*) and "part" or "side" (*parte*). William Buonaparte eventually settled in the Tuscan village of Sarzana, where the family remained for nearly three centuries before Francesco Buonaparte, a nobleman from Sarzana, migrated to Corsica by the early 1500s. Francesco was Carlo's great-great-great-great-great-great-grandfather.

The lineage linking Carlo to Francesco spanned for nearly three centuries. Carlo was the son of a Corsican politician named Nobile Giuseppe Maria Buonaparte or Giuseppe Maria di Buonaparte, who lived from 1713 to 1763. "Nobile" is generally defined as an Italian title of nobility ranking between knight and baron. Giuseppe's father was Nobile Sebastiano Nicola Buonaparte or Sebastiano Nicola di

Buonaparte, who was born in 1683. Sebastiano, like his father, grandfather, and great-grandfather, served as an elder of the Council of the City of Ajaccio. Sebastiano was the son of Giuseppe Maria Buonaparte, born 1663, who was the son of Carlo Maria Buonaparte, born 1637, who was the son of Sebastiano Buonaparte, born 1603. This Sebastiano was the son of Francesco Buonaparte, born around 1570, who served as an officer in the Republic of Genoa's military forces and as a "colonel commander" (a rank equivalent to "brigadier") of his own regiment in Corsica. Francesco was a son of the politician Geronimo Buonaparte, born around 1550, who served as head of the Council of Ajaccio. Geronimo was a son of Gabriele Buonaparte, who was a son of a senior Francesco Buonaparte, a nobleman who as a mercenary had been assigned to and then settled permanently in Corsica. He thereby founded the Corsican line of Buonapartes, of which the young schoolboy at Brienne was just one of many members.

Although it may be difficult to imagine a member of the nobility, let alone a future great conqueror, being the victim of bullying, that was the young Napoleon's reality. Cruel classmates transformed the Corsican version of his name, "Napoleone," into "Paille-au-Nez," or "Straw-nose."

The mainland French students teased him primarily for his Corsican accent. But despite being a subject of derision, Napoleon persevered by reading extensively, especially about history and geography. Among the works he read were Plutarch's *Lives*, translated from Latin to French, and Caesar's *Gallic War*. Such literary classics provided Napoleon with tales of heroic men he would later seek to emulate and even rival. It is therefore not surprising that Napoleon also displayed his growing talent as a military tactician by organizing what had to have been some of history's most awe-inspiring snowball fights. One of these mock battles was famously re-enacted in the opening sequence of Abel Gance's epic 1927 silent film *Napoléon*. Napoleon's accomplishments with these snowball fights were hardly the only signs of his abilities. A school inspector described the student like this: "Constitution, health excellent: character submissive, sweet, honest, grateful: conduct very regular . . . is worthy to enter the School at Paris." To this inspector, Napoleon shined in particular as a student of mathematics, causing him to think the boy might be best suited for the navy. Of course, Napoleon would not follow that recommendation. That is not to suggest he completely disregarded his superiors' opinions. After all, Napoleon later remembered several of his teachers fondly enough to reward them with pensions.

In addition to his wintry and academic triumphs, Napoleon was not always entirely alone as a student at Brienne. In 1782, for example, his parents came to see him, and in June 1784, Napoleon's father visited again. On this second trip, Carlo traveled with Napoleon's younger brother, Lucien, and younger sister, Elisa. In a letter about the visit to Carlo's uncle, the archdeacon of Ajaccio, Napoleon revealed his opinions of his brothers, Joseph and Lucien. Of the then 9-year-old Lucien, Napoleon wrote, "He shows plenty of talent and good intentions. It is to be hoped that he will turn out well. He is a big upstanding boy, quick and impulsive, and he is making a good start. He knows French well . . . ." Napoleon's opinion of Joseph, however, was far more critical. He first lamented that Joseph did not write their father often enough. Napoleon then declared Joseph "not strong enough to face the dangers of war," a young man whose "weak health doesn't allow him to bear the strain of foreign service," before accusing him of exhibiting "some signs of extravagance and frivolity." Napoleon was not entirely negative about his big brother, though. He did at least describe Joseph as "cheerful and good looking," but overall Napoleon expressed disappointment that Joseph's personality flaws would prevent him from achieving his intellectual potential. For example, Napoleon wrote that Joseph "is in Rhetoric, and could do better than any of us if he cared; for the Principal told my dear father that there wasn't a more talented Physicist, Rhetorician, or Philosopher in the whole school, or one who could produce a better composition." At the time when this letter was written, Joseph had been studying at Autun to become a priest, but he was now considering military service.

Napoleon predicted that his brother would make a better priest than a soldier. Lucien, however, remained at the military school at Brienne. In their adult years, Napoleon would have a much closer relationship with Joseph than with Lucien.

Having completed his studies at Brienne by 1784, Napoleon was admitted at the age of 15 to the elite École Militaire de Paris, the Military School of Paris. That institution was France's equivalent to the United Kingdom's Sandhurst or the United States' West Point. At this prestigious military college, Napoleon received the nickname "the Spartan." He trained to become an artillery officer and completed the two-year course in just one year. He did so while also becoming the École's first Corsican graduate. In completing his studies, he continued to excel at mathematics, but was less successful in studying languages and, oddly enough, at dancing. These deficiencies hardly take away from his accomplishment in completing all his studies so rapidly. His graduation, however, may have been bittersweet.

When he graduated in September 1785, he had just lost his father. Carlo died of stomach cancer earlier that year, in February. A letter to his mother captures Napoleon's sadness at the loss of his father, his affection towards his mother, and his eloquence as a writer:

> MY DEAR MOTHER,
>
> Now that time has somewhat calmed the first transports of my grief, I hasten to assure you of the gratitude with which your kindness has always inspired me. Console yourself, my dear mother; circumstances require this. We will redouble our solicitude, happy if we can, by our obedience, make up in some degree for the inestimable loss of a cherished husband. I terminate, my dear mother, by imploring you to calm your grief. My health is perfect, and I pray every day that Heaven may favor you in a similar way . . . .
>
> Your very humble and affectionate son,
> NAPOLEONE DE BUONAPARTE

From 1785 to 1790, the now fatherless Napoleon served as a second lieutenant in France's La Fère artillery regiment. He got his commission at age 16. In this capacity, he worked hard for little pay while quartered at Valence on the Rhone River. Nevertheless, he also encountered his first love and thereby a means of rest from a soldier's life. Many years later, Napoleon remembered this lady, Caroline de Colombier (later Caroline de Bressieux), for having, of all things, eaten cherries with him. Sometimes simple pleasures give us the most peace! Although she never married him, or even became engaged, his first love did, however, retain a connection with his family. She later became a lady-in-waiting to Napoleon's mother.

By May 1786, despite the distractions of soldiery and love, Napoleon exhibited melodramatic melancholy. He wrote:

> Always alone, even in the midst of people, I have withdrawn to my room to commune with myself and give free vent to my despondency. Whither do my thoughts turn today? To death. Yet my life is only at its dawn and I may expect to live a long time. I have been away from my native land between six and seven years. What a delight it will be to meet my compatriots and my dear ones again! From the sweet emotions roused by the memories of my childhood, may I not conclude that my happiness will be complete? What madness is it that urges me on to destruction? What indeed am I to do in the world? Since I must die some day, why not now? If I were a man of sixty I would respect the prejudices of my contemporaries and wait patiently till Nature had run her course. But since misfortune has met me on the very threshold of life and I have no delight in anything, why prolong such an existence? How far off men are from Nature! How cowardly, servile, and despicable! What sight awaits me in my native land? My countrymen, loaded with chains, kiss with trembling the hand that oppresses them. They are no longer the brave Corsicans whom a hero inspired with own virtues, no longer as of yore

> the enemy of tyrants and luxury and cringing courtiers . . . Frenchmen! Not content with having robbed us of what we valued most, you have corrupted our morals. The present condition of my country and my powerlessness to alter it, is only a fresh reason for me quitting a world where duty compels me to praise those whom virtue bids me despise. What could I do, suppose I were back in my native country? What could I say? When his country has ceased to be, nothing remains for a good citizen but to die. Were there only one life to be destroyed in order to free my compatriots, I would instantly hasten to plunge a dagger into the tyrant's breast and so avenge my country and these dishonoring laws. My life is a burden to me, for it holds out no prospect of pleasure, and everything seems to turn into a cause of sorrow because those with whom I live and shall probably always live are utterly unlike myself, as unlike as sunlight to moonlight. I cannot therefore lead the kind of life which alone would make existence bearable, and hence arises endless dissatisfaction with everything.

This despondent letter not only showcases Napoleon's dark mental state but also the conflict in loyalties between Corsica, his native land, and the nation in whose army he now served.

Despite serving with a French commission, his sympathies at this time clearly resided more with Corsica than with France. In fact, he spent well over a year in Corsica while on leave from his regiment. He revisited his homeland in September 1786 and did not return to his regiment, now stationed at Auxonne, for some 21 months. Before joining his regiment there in June 1788, he had spent several weeks in late 1787 in Paris, growing even further disillusioned with France's royal government. In October 1788, he sketched a *Dissertation on Royal Authority* in which he wrote, "This work will begin with general ideas as to the origin and the enhanced prestige of the name of king. Military rule is favorable to it: this work will afterwards enter into the details of the usurped authority enjoyed by the Kings of the twelve Kingdoms of Europe . . . . There are very few Kings who have not deserved dethronement." In May 1789, before revolutionary fervor had taken hold of France, Napoleon wrote in the manner of a Corsican revolutionary:

> As the nation was perishing I was born. Thirty thousand Frenchmen were vomited on to our shores, drowning the throne of liberty in waves of blood. Such was the odious sight which was the first to strike me. From my birth, my cradle was surrounded by the cries of the dying, the groans of the oppressed and tears of despair. You left our island and with you went all happiness. Slavery was the price of our submission. Crushed by the triple yoke of the soldier, the law-maker and the tax inspector, our compatriots lived despised.

Napoleon had written these words to none other than the Corsican nationalist Pasquale Paoli. He had been the president of the Corsican Republic from 1755 to 1769, but after suffering a decisive defeat in 1769 by French forces in the Battle of Ponte-Novo, he fled to England. He remained exiled there until 1790, not long after receiving Napoleon's letter.

Napoleon remained with his regiment at Auxonne until September 1789. Yet, despite being back in France, his thoughts remained focused on Corsica. He even worked on a history of the island and wrote again to Paoli, this time asking his opinion about some of Napoleon's writings and asking for various historical documents. Unfortunately for Napoleon, Paoli was not only unimpressed with Napoleon's effort at historical writing, but also refused to provide the requested documents. A rift developed between Napoleon and Paoli that would grow deeper during the French Revolution.

By 1789, the year in which the Revolution began, Napoleon turned 20, becoming an educated and passionate man. In those two decades, he had traveled back and forth between France and Corsica, interacting with Frenchmen and Corsicans alike. Among the major influences on his early life were his father's death and the end of Napoleon's youthful idolization of Paoli. Yet his mother remained an important part of his life, as she would for his entire career, which would be forged in the furnace of one of history's most tumultuous periods. This era of "French" Revolution would have consequences well beyond France's borders; the man most credited with spreading its influence across Europe and beyond would be the second surviving son of Letizia Bonaparte.

2. Napoleon and the French Revolution (1789-1798)

As French men and women fought for liberty, equality, and fraternity, Napoleon returned to Corsica where his conflict with Paoli became more pronounced. Now a captain in France's army, Napoleon supported the republican, Jacobin movement associated with the French Revolution, even organizing Jacobin activity on Corsica. Paoli, meanwhile, had been elected president of the French Department of Corsica, but he broke with France's revolutionary government in a rather spectacular manner.

The revolutionary government had ordered Paoli to take the nearby island of Sardinia. Paoli responded by putting his nephew in charge of the expedition, with secret orders to fail in his mission. Paoli also sent Napoleon, now a colonel in the Corsican National Guard as well as a French army officer in command of two companies. The Corsican guard was unofficially reinforced by 6,000 revolutionaries from Marseille. Napoleon's companies participated in an assault on Maddalena Island in 1793, but as Paoli had planned with his nephew, the overall invasion failed. Napoleon realized something nefarious was at play. He assumed command of the expedition, but it was too late. Defeated and betrayed, he and his entire family denounced Paoli as a traitor to the French National Convention. This did not deter the Paolists, who joined forces with the royalists, declared Napoleon an outlaw, and on June 10, 1793, drove him and his entire family from Corsica. Paoli then declared Corsica's secession from France and requested British protection. Britain responded by declaring a Corsican kingdom, with King George III as its king. His rule lasted only from 1794 to October 1796, when France regained control of the island. As for Paoli, he returned to England for the second exile in 1795, even before the French completed their reconquest of Corsica. He died in England in 1807, having failed ultimately to preserve Corsican independence. Napoleon, however, was hardly finished. Now embracing France, he became an increasingly important figure in the French Revolutionary government's effort to consolidate its revolution.

In July 1793, the same year as the failed assault on Maddalena Island and his subsequent expulsion from Corsica, Napoleon wrote a pro-republican pamphlet titled *Le Souper de Beaucaire* (Supper at Beaucaire). This literary endeavor attracted the attention of the younger brother of the infamous and allegedly incorruptible revolutionary leader Maximilien Robespierre. Soon enough, with Napoleon finding support among a leading faction of France's revolutionary government, he was appointed artillery commander of republican forces at the siege of Toulon. Napoleon earned recognition for his military genius in devising a plan to help win the siege for France. He fought bravely alongside his soldiers, suffering a wound to his thigh in the process. For this success, Napoleon became, at just 24 years of age, a brigadier general and commander of artillery for France's Army of Italy. In this position, he planned a French attack on the Kingdom of Sardinia. The invasion was successfully carried out by Pierre Dumerbion and the future Marshal of France André Masséna. Napoleon seemed poised for future opportunities to help win the war for the government led by Robespierre.

Yet, while Napoleon was busy with his military activities, Robespierre was leading France's Reign of Terror. During 1793 and 1794, tens of thousands had perished by guillotining or other summary executions. By July 27, 1794, members of the National Convention who had become fed up with Robespierre's excesses, voted to execute him and his allies. Napoleon endured arrest for a short period but was spared the fate of his former Jacobin supporters. This apparent stroke of luck likely occurred because he was in the south of France; had he been in Paris, his fate, and that of the world, would likely have been far different.

In 1795, Napoleon, now free from association with the deceased Robespierre brothers, experienced his next notable romantic relationship. He became engaged to a certain Désirée Clary. She was eight years younger than Napoleon and the sister of Julie Clary, who was married to Napoleon's elder brother, Joseph. Napoleon wrote a tragic romantic novella titled *Clisson and Eugénie* about a soldier and his lover that paralleled his own relationship with Désirée. Although that relationship did not have the exact ending that Napoleon composed for his novella's titular characters, his romance with Désirée was nonetheless short-lived. They were never married.

During the time of his romance with Désirée, Napoleon's prospects as a military commander seemed uncertain. On the one hand, he was assigned to the Army of the West, which at the time was engaged in the war in the Vendée. That was a civil war against a royalist counter-revolution that occurred between 1793 and 1796 in France's west-central Atlantic Coast region. Accepting this command would have required him to lead French soldiers against fellow Frenchmen. To avoid that posting, he pleaded poor health and instead was moved to the Committee of Public Safety's Bureau of Topography. In a great "what if" scenario, he actually sought a transfer to Constantinople so he could offer his services to the Sultan of Turkey. One can only imagine how modern history would have been altered had Napoleon spent his career working for the Ottoman Empire instead of France. For better or worse, this effort was unsuccessful. And so Napoleon, having refused to serve in the Vendée campaign, was removed from the list of generals in regular service.

With no command and facing financial difficulties, Napoleon needed some dramatic opportunity to catapult himself into prominence once again. As he noted, "Ability is of little account without opportunity." The opportunity that would set him on the path to becoming his age's most influential military leader came in 1795.

A period engraving of Paul Barras.

On October 3 of that year, royalists in Paris rose in a rebellion against the National Convention, essentially a counter-revolution against the Republican revolution. At this time, with both the former King Louis XVI and the revolutionary leader Robespierre long dead, a new man had come to lead France. This man, Paul Barras, who lived from 1755 to 1829, came to fame as a leader of what is known as the Thermidorian Reaction against Robespierre. Barras, familiar with Bonaparte's military triumph at Toulon, gave the young Corsican command of the improvised forces defending the Convention in the Tuileries Palace. The choice was good, because Napoleon, having seen the king's Swiss Guard massacred at the Tuileries three years earlier, understood that artillery would be the key to the palace's defense.

Bonaparte ordered a young cavalry officer named Joachim Murat (who later became Napoleon's brother-in-law), to seize cannons that could repel the attackers. The fateful attack occurred on October 5, 1795—also known as 13 Vendémiaire An IV in the French republican calendar. The republican forces consisted of some 5,000 men and 40 cannons, versus 25,000 to 30,000 royalists—a disadvantage of about six to one!

Despite being overwhelmingly outnumbered in manpower, Napoleon did have some things going in his favor. Superior discipline, possession of cannons, and leadership skills compensated for his numerical disadvantage. Concerning Napoleon's leadership, keep in mind that he was not just a brilliant tactician. In this street battle, he once again displayed personal bravery. He commanded his men throughout a two-hour engagement. In the ferocious fighting, he managed to survive relatively unharmed, despite having his horse shot from under him. The same could not be said for the royalists.

Certainly, a number of the attackers were brave, but they, unlike Napoleon, would not walk away from the battle unscathed. Napoleon's cannons fired grapeshot into the unfortunate massed royalists. Grapeshot is a mass of small metal balls packed tightly into a canvas bag, resembling a cluster of grapes. On firing, the balls spread out from the muzzle, akin to a super-sized shotgun. The devastating consequences of firing grapeshot into a mass of people include simultaneous mass infliction of serious, gruesome injuries. A single shot from a cannon, therefore, can accomplish what would otherwise require multiple soldiers firing a volley from muskets.

Ultimately, while Barras and Napoleon only lost about 100 dead and wounded, perhaps 300 to 1,400 royalists died. Two captured royalists were executed, and the rest fled. Forty years later, the 19th-century Scottish philosopher and historian Thomas Carlyle wrote in *The French Revolution: A History* that Napoleon had cleared the streets with "a whiff of grapeshot" and that "the thing we specifically call French Revolution is blown into space by it." To Carlyle, the events of 13 Vendémiaire mark the revolution's end. Indeed, from this moment on and until 1815, the history of France increasingly became the history of Napoleon Bonaparte.

Barras and Bonaparte's defeat of the royalist insurrection, therefore, did not just extinguish the threat to the Convention, but it also earned Napoleon considerable fame as a national hero. With fame came wealth and the patronage of the new government dominated by Barras and France's new executive body, the five-man Directory.

As for Murat, his star became linked to Napoleon's for the remainder of Murat's life. He would later marry one of Napoleon's sisters and also serve as one of Napoleon's better-known generals. He would eventually become one of Europe's best–and most flamboyant–cavalry commanders.

The defeated royalists would not see a king return to rule France for nearly 20 years. Moreover, in an unsuccessful attempt to portray the outnumbered Republicans' triumphant defense as a massacre, the royalist losers nicknamed Bonaparte "Général Vendémiaire." Rather than take offense, Napoleon later claimed this as his first title of glory.

Many more titles would soon follow.

For instance, in the aftermath of his "whiff of grapeshot," Bonaparte received a quick promotion to Commander of the Interior, and then commander of the Army of France in Italy. But before he would achieve his next military success, an affair of the heart that has captivated romantics for the past 200 years reminded the world of Napoleon's tender side.

1798 engraving of Napoleon's wife, Josephine de Beauharnais.

Within weeks of the events of early October 1795, Napoleon became romantically involved with Rose (later Josephine) de Beauharnais (1763-1814), the former mistress of Paul Barras. The couple married on March 9, 1796, in a civil ceremony.

Like Napoleon, Josephine had been born on an island, only in her case, it was Martinique in the Caribbean. She was the eldest daughter of a wealthy white Creole family that owned a sugarcane plantation. Unfortunately, hurricanes destroyed her family's estate in 1766. Nevertheless, an opportunity to restore the family's prestige came in 1779 when Alexandre, son of a French aristocrat François, Vicomte de Beauharnais, married Josephine in France. The couple had two children. Their son, Eugène de Beauharnais, born in 1781, would later become one of Napoleon's most loyal subordinates. Their daughter, Hortense de Beauharnais, born in 1783, married Napoleon's brother Louis Bonaparte in 1802, and was also intensely loyal to Napoleon.

The French Revolution proved particularly perilous for Alexandre and Josephine. In 1794, during the Reign of Terror, the Committee of Public Safety ordered the arrest of first Alexandre and later Josephine. Both endured imprisonment, but only Alexandre perished at the guillotine. Josephine narrowly avoided the same fate, being freed a mere five days after her husband's death, thanks to the fall and execution of Robespierre, which ended the Reign of Terror.

The now liberated Josephine became the lover of Barras, who was the leading political figure of the post-Reign of Terror. In 1795, she met his military ally, Napoleon Bonaparte. Although six years her junior, Napoleon became her new lover. His beautiful and moving words to Josephine once again reveal his tender side, as well as his talents as a writer. In one letter from December 1795, he wrote:

> I awake full of you. Your image and the memory of last night's intoxicating pleasures has left no rest to my senses.
>
> Sweet, incomparable Josephine, what a strange effect you have on my heart. Are you angry? Do I see you sad? Are you worried? My soul breaks with grief, and there is no rest for your lover; but how much the more when I yield to this passion that rules me and drink a burning flame from your lips and your heart? Oh! This night has shown me that your portrait is not you!
>
> You leave at midday; in three hours I shall see you.
>
> Meanwhile, my sweet love, a thousand kisses; but do not give me any for they set my blood on fire.

The next month, in January 1796, Napoleon proposed to her, and they married on March 9. As a fascinating result of their relationship, the bride adopted not only a new last name, but also a new first name. Before meeting Bonaparte, she had been known as Rose, but Bonaparte preferred to call her Josephine. Generally speaking, the general got what he wanted, and so we remember the great romance of Napoleon and Josephine, not Napoleon and Rose.

Josephine's in-laws were not exactly welcoming to this new addition to their clan. Napoleon's family felt shocked that he married an older widow with two children. The female members of his family also showed a bit of jealousy. His hard-living Corsican mother and sisters resented being in the presence of a woman who displayed more sophistication and social graces than they did.

In any case, Napoleon had more pressing matters to attend to than maintaining familial harmony. Just two days after the wedding, he left to lead a French army that would invade Italy. Nevertheless, Napoleon's thoughts lingered on his new bride. During their many months of separation, the conqueror of northern Italy continued to send her numerous love letters. In February 1797, he wrote, "You to whom nature has given spirit, sweetness, and beauty, you who alone can move and rule my heart, you who know all too well the absolute empire you exercise over it!" The sentiment, however, was not reciprocated. Left behind in Paris, Josephine began an affair in 1796 with a handsome Hussar lieutenant, Hippolyte Charles, who was roughly ten years her junior. When rumors of the relationship reached a now infuriated Napoleon, the nature of his love for her changed. To his dying day, he would still love her, but it was never the same as it had been that first year of their romance. As for Josephine's beau, he continued to serve in French armies and outlived both Napoleon and Josephine.

Amidst this marital tumult, Napoleon waged his campaign in Italy with a genius rarely exhibited in all of military history. Taking command of the Army of Italy to begin his first campaign of conquest, the modern Hannibal immediately went on the offensive. He intended to defeat the Piedmontese forces in northern Italy before any possible intervention by their Austrian allies. It took the audacious Napoleon a mere two weeks to defeat Piedmont's army before the French shifted their focus to the Austrians for the remainder of the campaign. The centerpiece of this campaign and one of the decisive battles of history was the siege of Mantua.

The Austrians launched many offensives against the French in an ultimately futile effort to break the siege. Napoleon defeated every one of these Austrian relief efforts. He scored victories at the battles of Castiglione in August 1796, Bassano in September, Arcole in November, and Rivoli in January 1797. This campaign inspired one of the most famous artistic depictions of Napoleon: the 1796 painting *Bonaparte at the Pont d'Arcole* by Antoine-Jean Gros.

Bonaparte at the Bridge of Arcole (1796) by Antoine-Jean Gros (1771–1835) reproduced here from Wikipedia.

It was at Arcole that Napoleon tried to inspire his men to attack by grabbing a flag and standing in the open on a dike about 55 paces from the bridge depicted in the painting. Although several members of his staff were hit by the intense fire and his aide-de-camp was killed, by a seeming miracle Napoleon was unharmed before an unknown officer dragged him into a muddy ditch out of the line of fire. Various works of art inaccurately show Napoleon on the bridge. Yet, even if the incident has been fictionalized in later artistic depictions, Napoleon's bravery in the actual moment should hardly be questioned.

A period engraving of Charles-Louis, Archduke Charles.

Napoleon did go on to win the battle, but Arcole was not the end of the war. The last of these four key victories and the decisive one, at Rivoli, led to the collapse of Austria's position in Italy. The toll of casualties reveals just how astonishing Napoleon's triumphs were. In these four battles alone, his army lost "only" 9,700 to 11,500 men, versus the horrifying Austrian losses of 21,200 to 23,200.

Yet Napoleon did not stop there. In the campaign's next phase, the French took the war to the Habsburg heartlands. Napoleon pushed back forces commanded by Austria's Archduke Charles, who would be Napoleon's future uncle-in-law. Napoleon advanced deep into Austrian territory after defeating Charles at the Battle of Tarvis in March 1797. France's Army of Italy lost 1,200 soldiers; the Austrian Army lost 4,500 men, 25 guns, and 400 to 500 wagons. Napoleon's success alarmed the Austrians. When his forces were just 75 miles from Vienna, Austria finally decided to sue for peace. The subsequent treaties concluded in October 1797 ended the war with Austria that had begun in 1792 and confirmed France's control of northern Italy. France also gained the Austrian Netherlands (Belgium), while the Republic of Venice was promised to Austria.

Napoleon recognized immediately that his victories would have far-reaching consequences for France and beyond. In October 1797, amid the treaty negotiations, he wrote from his headquarters in Passariano to the Minister for Foreign Affairs:

> It is a French characteristic to take prosperity much too lightly. Could we but base all our operations on a sound policy–by which I mean simply calculating *what* is likely to happen, and *when*, we might remain for a long time the greatest nation, and the arbiter of Europe. Nay more; we already hold the scales of power, and can incline them which way we will; indeed, I see nothing to prevent our reaching, in a few years' time, if fate wills it so, results which only burning enthusiasm can envisage, and only a man of cool and reasoned constancy can attain.

Bonaparte followed up his victory over Austria by marching on Venice. The watery city's surrender ended over 1,000 years of independence. As a further insult, French forces looted such Venetian treasures as the four bronze horse statues on Saint Mark's Basilica (though to be fair, they were already stolen property. Venice had looted them from Constantinople in 1204). That was hardly the only example of French appropriation of other nations' wealth. For instance, over the course of his awe-inspiring Italian campaign in 1796 and 1797, Bonaparte's French army fought 67 actions, won 18 pitched battles, and captured 150,000 prisoners, 540 cannons, and 170 standards. His forces also extracted about $45 million in cash from Italy, another $12 million in precious metals and jewels, and more than 300 priceless paintings and sculptures.

Bonaparte returned to Paris in December 1797 as a conquering hero. In the capital, he met Charles-Maurice de Talleyrand, France's new foreign minister, who would later serve in the same capacity for Emperor Napoleon. With a major continental threat to republican France defeated, the two men prepared to deal with France's chief seaborne enemy, Britain. The question now became: would Napoleon follow in the footsteps of William the Conqueror and invade Britain or would he, perhaps, seek to emulate the much earlier conqueror, Alexander the Great, and take an alternate path to glory?

3. Napoleon as Alexander (1798-1799)

While in exile on St. Helena in November 1816, Napoleon remarked that "Alexander, when scarcely beyond the age of boyhood, with a mere handful of troops, conquered a quarter of the globe." Napoleon was factually wrong; as any map of Alexander's empire would reveal, he did *not* conquer a quarter of the world (though the territory he seized did spread over 3,000 miles south and east of his native Macedonia). Nevertheless, Bonaparte's fascination with the ancient conqueror is obvious. Napoleon went on to ask, "But was this achievement the result of a mere accidental irruption? No; all was profoundly calculated, boldly executed, and prudently managed. Alexander proved himself at once a distinguished warrior, politician and legislator." Over the course of Napoleon's career, he too would prove himself a distinguished warrior, politician, and legislator, often playing these roles simultaneously. His leadership of the expedition to Egypt in 1798 and 1799 was one such instance.

1796 engraving by Chapman of Alexander the Great.

Before the Egyptian campaign began, France's government and the expedition's future commander offered different rationales for undertaking such a bold venture. The Directory's reasons for the campaign included an admission that an invasion of Britain would be premature, an attempt to threaten the British colony India, and a means of getting the popular Bonaparte out of the way. Indeed, one might speculate that they wanted him to be a great success but die in the process! As for Napoleon's rationale for the campaign, he wanted to get out of the way while the Directory self-destructed; he too wanted to threaten India; and, finally, he toyed with the idea of perhaps even taking down the Ottoman Empire.

The British response to military movements in and around France was intended to protect the English Channel, prevent another French attempt to invade Ireland, and safeguard British interests in the Eastern Mediterranean and India. Although the French offensive in Egypt is fairly well known today, France's attacks across the English Channel and against British control of Ireland are largely forgotten. The significance of these attacks at the time, however, should not be neglected in understanding the broader strategic situation while Napoleon was meandering through the Mediterranean in 1798 and 1799.

Although Napoleon invaded Egypt rather than England, the French Republic did, in fact, attempt a small-scale landing in Wales in 1797 with the aim of marching on Bristol, England. A small French force of about 1,400, led by the Irish-American William Tate, came ashore at Fishguard in February 1797. Tate was a veteran of the American war for independence from Britain. The subsequent Battle of Fishguard, from February 22 to 24, 1797, is notable as the most recent effort by any foreign force to land in Britain, and thus is considered the "last invasion of Britain." While British losses were light, the French side had 33 killed and wounded; 1,360 captured, including Tate; and two ships—a frigate and corvette—seized.

Earlier, in December 1796, the French had unsuccessfully attempted to help the Society of United Irishmen in a planned rebellion against British rule. The attempt was a disaster for both the French republicans and Irish rebels. The French fleet was partially destroyed by a storm, and the expedition failed. Of 44 ships, 12 were captured or wrecked. Of the estimated 15,000 to

20,000 soldiers, sailors, and marines, 2,230 were killed or drowned, and another 1,000 were captured. Nevertheless, on August 22, 1798, about 1,000 French soldiers under General Jean Joseph Amable Humbert landed at Kilcummin in County Mayo in the northwest of Ireland. They were soon joined by approximately 5,000 Irish rebels and enjoyed some initial success. Despite being outnumbered 6,000 to 2,000, the French and the United Irishmen inflicted a humiliating defeat on the British in the Battle of Castlebar on August 27, 1798. French and Irish casualties were 150 dead and wounded, versus 80 British dead and another 270 wounded, captured, or deserted. The victors then set up a short-lived "Republic of Connacht," which lasted just from August 27 to September 8, 1798, under President John Moore. The French General Humbert was named commander-in-chief of the Army of Ireland. This success sparked some supportive risings in Longford and Westmeath, but these were quickly defeated. The British then won a decisive victory over the French and United Irishmen in the battle of Ballinamuck, in County Longford, on September 8. The victors had only about 12 dead and 16 wounded, while the losers suffered losses of about 500 killed and another 1,144 captured. The French troops who surrendered, including General Humbert, were repatriated to France, but hundreds of the captured Irish rebels were executed. Ex-president Moore was tried and sentenced to be transported to the penal colony in Australia, but died before the sentence could be carried out. On October 12, 1798, an even larger French force consisting of 3,000 men attempted to land near Lough Swilly in County Donegal. This force included Theobald Wolfe Tone, co-founder of the Society of United Irishmen. This third attempt by the republican French to disrupt British rule of Ireland never even touched Irish soil. The Franco-Irish force was intercepted by a larger Royal Navy squadron and surrendered after the three-hour Battle of Tory Island. That lopsided battle saw 150 British casualties versus 700 French, plus another 2,400 French captured and the loss of seven French ships. Wolfe Tone was tried by court-martial in Dublin and found guilty. He asked for death by firing squad, but when this request was refused, Tone slit his throat on November 12, 1798. He died a week later.

Thus, Napoleon's struggle in Egypt, this period's main event, was but part of a much larger conflict, a world war of sorts. Napoleon could well have repeated the failures of the abortive invasions of Britain and Ireland. In fact, on October 27, 1797, he had been given the command of an army to invade England. During the winter that followed, he spent some two months planning for this invasion before deciding that France's naval power was not yet strong enough to confront the British Royal Navy. On February 23, 1798, Napoleon wrote to the Executive Directory:

> Whatever efforts we make, it will still be many years before we achieve supremacy at sea. To carry out an invasion of England without command of the sea is as difficult and daring a project as has ever been undertaken. It could only be done by a surprise crossing–either by eluding the fleet that is blockading Brest and the Texel, or by landing in small boats, during the night after a 7 or 8 hours' passage, at some point in the counties of Kent or Sussex. This operation requires long nights, and therefore wintertime. It can't be attempted later than April. Any such invasion by means of sloops during a calm spell in the summer is impracticable: the enemy would offer insuperable obstacles to our embarkation, and still more to our passage. Our fleet is no further advanced than it was when we mobilized the army of invasion, four months ago . . . . The English expedition therefore seems to me impossible until next year; and then it is likely to be prevented by fresh embarrassments on the continent. The real moment for preparing this invasion has passed, perhaps forever . . . .
>
> We should therefore give up any real attempt to invade England, and content ourselves with the appearance of it, whilst devoting all our attention and resources to the Rhine, so as to deprive England of Hanover and Hamburg. It is

admitted that, if we are to achieve both aims, we must not keep a large army at a distance from Germany.

Or we might well make an expedition into the Levant, and threaten the commerce of India.

In conclusion, Napoleon decided instead on a military expedition to seize Egypt and undermine Britain's access to its trade interests in India. To that end, he wished not only to establish a French presence in the Near East but also to link up with Tipu Sultan of Mysore, a Muslim potentate who was an enemy of the British in India and a pioneer in the use of rocket artillery. Thus, Napoleon informed the Directory that "as soon as he had conquered Egypt, he will establish relations with the Indian princes and, together with them, attack the English in their possessions." The Directory agreed with his planned expedition in order to secure a French trade route to India, but before the directors would send him off to his next adventure, another remarkable moment occurred in Napoleon's career.

In May 1798, he once again showed himself to be more than just an incredibly successful general: he was elected a member of the French Academy of Sciences. With his devotion to the sciences and Enlightenment principles, the Egyptian expedition would not be a merely military affair. In addition to a military force of 40,000 soldiers and 10,000 sailors in a large fleet of 13 ships of the line, 14 frigates, and 400 transports, 167 scholars were assigned to the expedition. Among these were mathematicians, naturalists, chemists, and even geodesists–scientists who study the measurement and representation of the Earth or any planet, as well as engineers and other technical specialists. Before addressing their accomplishments, let us first examine the course of the French fleet's odyssey from Toulon, France to Alexandria, Egypt.

On May 9, 1798, Bonaparte arrived at Toulon. Ten days later, on May 19, he addressed his troops:

Soldiers! You are one of the wings of the Army of England; you have made war in mountains, plains, and cities; it remains to make it on the ocean. The Roman legions, whom you have often imitated but not yet equaled, combated Carthage, by turns, on the seas and on the plains of Zama. Victory never deserted their standards, because they never ceased to be brave, patient and united. Soldiers! The eyes of Europe are upon you; you have great destinies to accomplish; battles to fight; dangers and fatigues to overcome; you are about to do more than you have yet done for the prosperity of your country, the happiness of man, and your own glory. The genius of liberty, which has rendered, from its birth, the Republic the arbiter of Europe, has now determined that it should become so of the seas, and of the most distant nations.

1798 engraving of Napoleon in Malta. Note the British spelling 'Buonaparte.'

On June 9, 1798, the French fleet reached the island of Malta, then controlled by the Knights of St John. Their grandmaster surrendered after token resistance. With the loss of only three men, Bonaparte had captured an important naval base between France and Egypt. While he was at it, he rewrote Malta's constitution, deported the Knights, reorganized the educational system, gave religious freedom to the Jews, and abolished feudalism and slavery. Not a bad week's work!

Next, Bonaparte's expedition continued to elude pursuit by the British Royal Navy, landing in Alexandria on July 1. From there, the French conquest of Egypt would begin.

A gold snuffbox showing General Bonaparte at the Battle of the Pyramids. The box is from somewhat later as it shows his generals wearing the uniform of the Imperial Guard (1805 forward).

First, on July 13, Bonaparte's army fought Murad Bey's Mamluks at the Battle of Shubra Khit. Although Egypt was nominally part of the Ottoman Empire, its actual ruling military caste was a native group called the Mamluks. This early victory helped the French practice their defensive tactics for the subsequent Battle of the Pyramids on

July 21. Despite the name, it was actually fought about 15 miles from the pyramids. Napoleon reportedly motivated his troops by telling them that "forty centuries look down upon you." In this second battle, the French won a decisive victory, thousands of Egyptians having lost their lives versus just 29 French. That lopsided victory boosted the morale of a French army fighting so far from its homeland.

The way Napoleon went about attempting to conquer the hearts and minds of Egyptians before, during, and after these triumphs may be shocking to those who see him solely as a military personage. Despite the sometimes-negative portrayals of Napoleon as a warmongering tyrant, in many respects, he was a humanitarian.

Napoleon instructed his army on how they should act toward Muslims: "Treat their Muftis and their Imams with respect, as you did the Rabbis and the Bishops." Concerning women, Napoleon explained, "The people among whom we are going treat women differently from us; but in every country, he who violates them is a monster!" In 1798, in Egypt, Napoleon also wrote that the "barbarous custom of whipping men suspected of having important secrets to reveal must be abolished. It has always been recognized that this method of interrogation, by putting men to the torture, is useless. The wretches say whatever comes into their heads and whatever they think one wants to believe. Consequently, the Commander-in-Chief forbids the use of a method which is contrary to reason and humanity." Finally, one can hardly forget the image of an almost Christ-like Napoleon immortalized in the 1804 painting *Bonaparte Visiting the Plague Victims of Jaffa* by Antoine-Jean Gros. The painting depicts a scene that occurred on March 11, 1799, in which, as the title suggests, Napoleon risked his own well-being by visiting plague-stricken soldiers.

"Bonaparte Visiting the Pesthouse in Jaffa" (1804) *by Antoine-Jean Gros (1771–1835) is reproduced here from Wikipedia.*

Beyond these orders and practices, many of Napoleon's other accomplishments in Egypt were more humanist than humanitarian. The Commission of the Sciences and Arts was a French learned body set up on March 16, 1798. Of its 167 members, all but 16 joined Bonaparte's invasion of Egypt. More than half were engineers and technicians, including 21 mathematicians, four astronomers, 17 civil engineers, 13 naturalists and mining engineers, geographers, three gunpowder engineers, four architects, eight artists, 10 mechanical artists, one sculptor, 15 interpreters, 10 men of letters, and 22 printers in Latin, Greek and Arabic characters. Napoleon, in turn, formed L'Institut d'Égypte as a learned academy to carry out research during his Egyptian campaign. It first met on August 24, 1798, with Bonaparte himself as vice-president. Later, on July 15, 1799, French soldiers discovered the first ancient multilingual Egyptian text recovered in modern times: The Rosetta Stone. Their work was published in the *Description de l'Égypte* in 1809.

If Napoleon approached his invasion as a man of the Enlightenment, then what prevented him from maintaining control of Egypt? His failure was mostly due to one battle and one siege.

In the first case, there was the Battle of Aboukir Bay, also known as the Battle of the Nile. On August 1, 1798, the British fleet under Admiral Horatio Nelson captured or destroyed most of Napoleon's ships, thereby virtually cutting him off from France. Nelson's annihilation of the French fleet disrupted Bonaparte's entire plan, defeating his goal of easily strengthening France's position in the Mediterranean. The French army in Egypt was now isolated from its homeland and surrounded by an actively hostile population. Deprived of its naval support and facing repeated uprisings, the army would attempt to break out of Egypt by land.

In early 1799, Napoleon moved part of his army into the Ottoman province of Damascus, the modern-day states of Syria, Lebanon, and Israel. Experiencing initial success, Bonaparte led his 13,000 soldiers to capture the coastal towns of Arish, Gaza, Jaffa, and Haifa. The attack on Jaffa was particularly brutal. Bonaparte discovered that many of the defenders were former prisoners of war, ostensibly on parole. The outraged general ordered the execution of 1,400 prisoners by bayonet or drowning to save bullets. His justifications for this directive were that he had neither the men nor supplies to keep them as prisoners, and that they had broken their vow not to take up arms for a year. Bonaparte had begun with an army of 13,000 men, but had lost 1,500 reported missing, 1,200 dead in combat, and thousands more who perished from disease, mostly bubonic plague. This land campaign culminated in the second military disaster Napoleon faced during the expedition: the siege of Acre.

From March 20 to May 21, 1799, the French besieged the ancient walled city of Acre, defended by an Ottoman garrison. The Ottoman land forces were supported by the British ships HMS *Theseus* and HMS *Tigre*. The defenders had 30,000 men to Napoleon's 9,000. On April 16, with a mere 4,000 men left, the French managed to defeat an Ottoman relief force of about 35,000 at the Battle of Mount Tabor. Ottoman losses were 6,000 killed and 500 captured versus only two French killed and 60 wounded. The French captured the entire baggage train. The Mamluks were finished as a fighting force. Nevertheless, 12,000 Ottoman reinforcements arrived to support Acre's defenders on May 7. Severely outnumbered, Napoleon failed to take the fortress. In the attempt, his army suffered casualties of 2,300 killed and 2,200 wounded or ill.

The siege proved a turning point in Napoleon's Egyptian expedition. One may wonder what the consequences may have been for history had the French captured Acre in 1799. Napoleon's assessment in 1805 may have been unrealistic, but it does reveal what he had hoped:

> If I had been able to take Acre, I would have put on a turban, I would have made my soldiers wear big Turkish trousers, and I would have exposed them to battle only in case of extreme necessity. I would have made them into a Sacred Battalion my Immortals. I would have finished the war against the Turks with Arabic, Greek, and Armenian troops . . . . I would have won a battle at Issus, I would have made myself emperor of the East, and I would have returned to Paris by way of Constantinople.

Napoleon's allusions from classical antiquity refer to the Sacred Band of Thebes and the Persian Immortals, elite units of the Greek city-state of Thebes and Persia's Achaemenid kings; and to the Battle of Issus in 333 B.C. where Alexander the Great decisively defeated the Persians.

Instead, battered and beaten after failing to take Acre, Napoleon would march his army not northward to Constantinople but southward, back to Egypt. Before undertaking that depressing return journey, he ordered that his plague-stricken men be euthanized by opium poisoning. The number who died remains disputed, ranging from 30 to as many as 580. This was intended as an act of mercy to protect them from likely Ottoman atrocities. Back in Egypt on July 25, Bonaparte defeated an Ottoman amphibious invasion at Aboukir, but his situation was not exactly hopeful. The circumstances back home were not good, either.

In Europe, France had suffered a series of defeats in what is known as the War of the Second Coalition. Having received word of these disasters, Napoleon took advantage of the temporary departure of British ships from French coastal ports and set sail for France on August 24, 1799. He left the army in Egypt in the charge of his general, Jean Baptiste Kléber. He proved a capable successor, winning a victory over the Ottoman Empire in the Battle of Heliopolis on March 20, 1800, but succumbed to an assassin's dagger a few months later. The third commander of the French army in Egypt, Jacques-François de Menou, married the daughter of a rich Egyptian, converted to Islam, and was renamed, Abdallah. Menou held out in Egypt for more than a year before surrendering to the British at the end of the siege of Alexandria, which lasted from August 17 to September 2, 1801. Ultimately, neither Bonaparte, Kléber, nor Menou, having fled, been murdered, or surrendered, would become a new Alexander the Great.

Nevertheless, many years after his Egyptian expedition, Napoleon reflected upon Alexander's example, remarking, "Unfortunately, on attaining the zenith of glory and success," the ancient warrior's "head was turned, and his heart corrupted. He commenced his career with the mind of Trajan; but he closed it with the heart of Nero, and the manners of Heliogabalus." At the end of 1799, Napoleon too would swap roles from one ancient leader to another. He would not become a Nero or Heliogabalus, but would seek to emulate Gaius Julius Caesar.

4. Napoleon as Caesar (1799-1804)

Soon after returning from Egypt, Napoleon traded his role as an Alexander the Great attempting to conquer the East, for that of a Julius Caesar transforming a republic into an empire. After all, as first consul, a revived Roman title, Napoleon even boasted: "I am descended from the best type of Caesars, that which founds." Of course, like Caesar, Napoleon had enemies within his own circles, and like Caesar, was the object of assassination plots, from both Royalist and Jacobin enemies. Fortunately for Bonaparte, those plots did not lead to the same conclusion that Caesar had suffered. In fact, Napoleon used these intrigues to justify a transition to an imperial system modeled on Ancient Rome, which included crowning himself emperor.

17th-century engraving of Julius Caesar by Agostini.

To that end, when Napoleon returned to France, he first had to seize control of and then form a new government. On November 9, 1799, he came to power in the coup of 18 Brumaire, which is generally recognized as the end of the French Revolution. Napoleon had used the ruse of "protecting" the directors from a non-existent Jacobin plot, persuading some to resign, but resorting to force to seize power from those who did not leave voluntarily. When addressing The Council of 500, Napoleon was physically assaulted by some of the delegates in an attempt to declare him an outlaw. Bonaparte asserted his seizure of power through the force of his loyal Grenadiers under the command of Joachim Murat, thus ending the opposition to his coup. Just over a month later, on December 24, 1799, a short and obscure Constitution was prepared under which Napoleon, as first consul, would have jurisdiction over the other two lesser consuls. Allowed to rule by decree, Napoleon effectively became the head of the French executive branch and the leader of France, but his reforming instincts were clear from the beginning. He insisted on universal male suffrage, making France even more democratic than the United States of America, where many of the states had property requirements for voting.

From 1800 to 1802, this new French government ended the Second Coalition that had fought against France, concluding the French Revolutionary War. The Treaty of Lunéville ended the conflict between France and the Holy Roman Empire in 1802, while The Peace of Amiens signed a year later finally brought peace between France and Britain. The peace was mostly a victory for France, which retained some of its conquests in Europe, despite having lost Egypt. Perhaps most importantly, France survived as a republic–of sorts–in a sea of monarchies.

The peace, however, only meant appeasement among the European powers. On the other side of the Atlantic, meanwhile, the Haitian Revolution that had begun in 1791 continued to claim French soldiers' lives. That colonial conflict, which lasted until 1804, served as a black mark on Napoleon's otherwise praiseworthy consular period.

In August 1791, the slaves in the French colony of Saint-Domingue had risen in revolt. During a night-time, religious ceremony on August 14, a high priest of voodoo gave the signal to begin the rebellion. Within the next 10 days, slaves took control of the entire Northern Province and "wreaked vengeance on their masters with pillage, rape, torture, mutilation, and death." Within weeks, 100,000 slaves joined the revolt, as the violence continued to escalate. These slaves killed some 4,000 whites and burned or destroyed hundreds of coffee, indigo, and sugar plantations. The French and Napoleon would find, just as Caesar, the Romans, and every other empire builder throughout history had, that subjugated people were an uneasy lot to manage, a simmering pot waiting to boil over.

By 1792, the slaves had not just thrown off their chains, but also controlled a third of the island of Hispaniola, on which Saint-Domingue is located. Their success caused the newly elected Legislative Assembly in France to grant, the spring of 1792, civil and political rights to free men of color in the colonies in an attempt to protect France's economic interests. The Legislative Assembly also appointed the abolitionist Léger-Felicité Sonthanax as revolutionary commissioner to assist the planters and free blacks in suppressing the slave revolts and preventing Spanish incursions into the colony.

Not surprisingly, slave-holding countries in Europe and the Americas were disturbed by the Legislative Assembly's decision. After all, Britain would not abolish slavery until 1833, and the United States of America not until 1865. Nevertheless, members of France's Legislative Assembly were willing to take a bold step toward eventual abolition decades before other powers did, if that was what it took to stop the rebellion. Yet granting rights to free people of color was only one measure French legislators undertook to resolve the crisis. The Legislative Assembly also sent 6,000 French soldiers to the island.

These soldiers would have more than slaves to contend with. When they arrived, they faced a multifaceted war that drew in two other European powers with colonial interests in the Caribbean: Spain and Great Britain. The French colony of Hispaniola was only on the western third of the island; Spain controlled the rest. And so, in 1793, when France declared war on Great Britain, Spain also joined the conflict and fought with Britain against France. Spanish forces invading Saint-Domingue were joined by slave forces. By August 1793, only 3,500 French soldiers remained on the island.

By January 29, 1794, a Spanish expedition seized Fort-Liberté, then named Fort-Dauphin, from France. The French colonial garrisons, with more than 1,000 men and 41 artillery guns, surrendered without firing a shot.

To prevent further military disaster, France's National Convention formally abolished slavery in 1794, more than 70 years before the United States would do so. The Convention also granted civil and political rights to all black men in the colonies. As a result, a liberated Creole slave and leader of the Haitian Revolution, François-Dominique Toussaint Louverture, sometimes called "The Black Napoleon," allied with the French Republic against the recalcitrant planters.

Unfortunately for Louverture, the French Republicans on the island did not share his vision for a peaceful resolution of the Haitian crisis. For example, Louverture reported the following conversation he had in 1797 with Léger-Félicité Sonthonax, an abolitionist and Jacobin who commanded the French troops:

> Commissioner Sonthonax: Do you know what we are going to do first? The blacks are worried for their freedom. We have here colonists of whom they are suspicious. They must all be slaughtered. Everything is ready. You only have to be in agreement with me.
>
> General Toussaint: What? You want to slaughter all the whites? Aren't you white yourself?
>
> Commissioner Sonthonax: Yes, but not all of them. Only those who are enemies of freedom . . . .
>
> General Toussaint: You mean, commissioner, that you want to ruin me . . . . Kill the whites? Take our independence? Did you not promise me that you'd never again talk of these projects?
>
> Commissioner Sonthonax: Yes, but you see it's absolutely indispensable . . .
>
> General Toussaint: . . . But if a white was killed here it is I

> who would be held responsible. I'm leaving, commissioner . . . . Commissioner, I am angry with you.

In August 1797, shortly after this conversation, Louverture expelled Sonthonax from Saint-Domingue.

Over the next few years, Louverture found himself in a bloody rivalry for leadership of the Haitian Revolution. The struggle, known as the War of Knives, pitted Louverture against a mulatto named Benoit Joseph André Rigaud in 1799 and 1800. Rigaud, who was born in 1761, had joined a brigade of volunteers that went to North America in 1779 to fight in the American Revolutionary War. As a commander of Haitian forces, Rigaud had won a significant victory over the British invasion, but Louverture outranked him in the French Army. To make matters worse, unlike Louverture, Rigaud, a light-skinned man of mixed racial ancestry, believed in perpetuating a race-based caste system that would put mulattoes just below whites while leaving blacks at the bottom. A French soldier and diplomat sent to the island named Gabriel-Marie-Théodore-Joseph, Comte d'Hédouville, further encouraged the animosity between Rigaud and Louverture to "divide and conquer" the non-white leaders on the islands. Ultimately, the rebels, led by Rigaud, were forced to make their final stand at Jacmel, which fell to Louverture in March 1800. Shortly afterward, Rigaud was exiled to France and Louverture had consolidated his position as leader.

By this time, Napoleon was in power in France, and Louverture hoped Napoleon would share his vision for Haiti. He even addressed a letter to Napoleon that began, "From the first of the blacks to the first of the whites." Nevertheless, as the husband of Josephine, a woman who came from a slave-owning family in the West Indies, Napoleon naturally had greater sympathies toward the white French slave-owners than the island's blacks.

Thus, Louverture faced full-on military opposition from France in the form of forces Napoleon sent to the island, commanded by Charles Victor Emmanuel Leclerc, a French Army general. Leclerc was married to Napoleon's sister Pauline Bonaparte.

On December 14, 1801, a French fleet of 21 frigates and 35 ships of the line left France carrying 7,000 to 8,000 troops. It would be followed by another squadron that sailed on February 14, 1802, with 4,200 troops. Another 2,400 troops left Cadiz on February 17, and still, more ships left France in the following months with fresh troops, including over 4,000 men from the Artillerie de Marine, a Dutch division, and the Polish Danube Legion. Spain also sent a fleet of seven ships. Considerable financial and material aid also came from Spanish Cuba. In total, 31,131 troops landed on Saint-Domingue, including some black figures such as André Rigaud. Napoleon sent Rigaud to unseat his old rival Louverture and re-establish both French colonial rule and slavery in Saint-Domingue. Another key commander of the French expedition also had a connection to the American Revolution. That was Donatien-Marie-Joseph de Vimeur, Vicomte de Rochambeau, born in 1755, who was the son of Jean-Baptiste Donatien de Vimeur, Comte de Rochambeau. The elder Rochambeau, born in 1725, had served as commander-in-chief of the French Expeditionary Force that helped the American Continental Army defeat British forces in Virginia in 1781.

The French expedition landed in December 1801. On February 23, 1802, Rochambeau defeated Louverture in the Battle of Snake Gully. From March 4 until March 24, 1802, Leclerc won a pyrrhic victory in the Battle of Crête-à-Pierrot. On March 12, when the French forces attempted to seize the Crête-à-Pierrot fort, they not only failed, but also suffered losses of 480 compared to the defenders' 200-300. The French lost another 300 dead during another failed attempt on March 22. The French finally took the fort when the Haitian rebels abandoned it on March 24. The French had gained the fort at the cost of hundreds of their soldiers, including the death of a general. Given the ratio of French soldiers on the island to Haitians, the French could not afford to lose so many in one battle. Nevertheless, the French would soon accomplish a major success when their general Jean Baptiste Brunet arrested Louverture on June 7. On July 2, 1802, Louverture arrived in France and on August 25 was placed in prison. By that time, the Law of May 20, 1802, had re-established slavery in France's colonies, revoking the Law of February 4, 1794.

With the black Haitians facing such serious reverses, it appeared that Napoleon might have been able to win an empire in the West and even invade North America, but one of the most horrible and unnecessary creatures in existence, virus-transmitting *Aedes aegypti* mosquito, would decide this conflict's fate. The combination of diseases it caused, mainly yellow fever and malaria, and the Haitians' continued brutal resistance turned Napoleon's dreams of restoring French power in the Caribbean into a nightmare. In fact, after only five months of Napoleon's campaign to reassert slavery in Haiti, 24,000 of the 40,000 French troops on the island were dead, and another 8,000 disabled, nearly all from disease.

An early 19th-century engraving entitled *Revenge Taken by the Black Army* shows black Haitian soldiers hanging white French soldiers, illustrating both the violence and the racial dimensions of the upheaval in Haiti. In fact, it is estimated that 100,000 blacks and 24,000 whites died in the slave rebellion. Even Charles Leclerc, Napoleon's brother-in-law and leader of the French force, was dead of yellow fever by November 1802. His wife, Pauline, who had accompanied him to Haiti, also suffered from spells of yellow fever, but she survived until dying of tuberculosis in 1825. After the failure of the Saint-Domingue expedition, Napoleon imprisoned Rigaud just a few cells away from Louverture himself. In 1803, Louverture died in prison of unknown causes. Rigaud returned to Haiti in 1810 and died there a year later.

"Revenge taken by the Black Army for the Cruelties practised on them by the French" is an illustration by British soldier and self-admitted "admirer of Toussaint L'Ouverture" Marcus Rainsford from his 1805 book An historical account of the black empire of Hayti reproduced here from Wikipedia.

The bloodshed in Haiti would, however, lead to two developments with global significance: The Louisiana Purchase of 1803 and Haitian Independence in 1804.

During the war in Haiti, American President Thomas Jefferson wanted to secure the area surrounding the valuable port of New

Orleans—constituting about half of the modern state of Louisiana—from French or Spanish control. To that end, Jefferson corresponded with Napoleon and sent ambassadors (including future U.S. President James Monroe) to negotiate. Jefferson was prepared to pay up to $10 million for this modest-sized territory. Had Napoleon's forces been able to consolidate control of and prevent the independence of Haiti, perhaps they would have been in a position, as Napoleon planned, to send forces to occupy the vast Louisiana territory. Alas, having suffered such horrendous losses and with war against Britain once again looming, Napoleon understood that he could not effectively occupy the Louisiana territory. He was better off, he concluded, allowing the better-positioned Americans to defend Louisiana against possible British attacks while also earning a modest sum of money from its sale. Thus, Napoleon made the U.S. envoys an amazing offer: he would sell them the entire Louisiana Territory, extending to the Rocky Mountains, for about $15 million. The American ambassadors signed the Louisiana Purchase Treaty more than two months before news of the deal reached Washington, D.C. The U.S. Senate ratified the treaty by a 24-7 vote, and the House of Representatives passed legislation authorizing the funds to acquire the new territory by a narrow margin of just 59 to 57. Thus, 23 percent of what we now know as the United States of America, including 14 of those states, stretching from New Orleans to Michigan in the East and Idaho in the west, was acquired in a single transaction for about $15 million.

The second major outcome of the Haitian Revolution was that by 1804, Haiti had won its independence from France. But instead of being some sort of democracy or republic in the model of the United States, Haiti became a horrifying empire ruled by another self-proclaimed emperor, Jean-Jacques Dessalines. Formerly a chief lieutenant to Louverture, he had risen to the rank of brigadier general by 1799. By the end of 1802, with Rigaud now siding with the French and Louverture captured, Dessalines was the rebels' most prominent remaining leader, which allowed him to consolidate command of the Haitian forces. He defeated the French in the decisive Battle of Vertières on November 18, 1803. This last major battle of the Second War of Haitian Independence was also the final part of the Haitian Revolution. On December 4, 1803, what remained of Napoleon's French colonial army in Haiti surrendered to Dessalines's forces, ending the only slave rebellion ever to establish an independent nation successfully; however, these victorious former slaves were not satisfied with their independence. They also sought violent revenge against their former masters, and anyone left on the island who even resembled them.

At the orders of Dessalines, now calling himself Jacques I, the black population carried out a genocidal massacre against Haiti's remaining whites consisting of native Frenchmen and French Creoles. The massacre took place in 1804 throughout Haiti, killing 3,000 to 5,000 people of all ages. An especially chilling 1806 engraving depicts Dessalines as a general with a sword raised in one hand, while the other holds a white woman's severed head. Whites who were spared included Polish mercenaries who had deserted from the French army, German colonists, and some medical doctors and their staffs.

Entitled simply "Desalines" (1806) by Manuel López López Iodibo, this image depicting the general, sword raised in one arm, while the other holds a severed head of a white woman reproduced here from Wikipedia.

Napoleon failed to achieve peace and stability in Haiti, but had greater success back home, even achieving religious peace in his authoritarian state. First, he dealt harshly with a particularly infamous atheist, Marquis Donatien Alphonse-François de Sade, ordering his arrest in 1801. Two years later, the Marquis de Sade was declared insane and transferred to an asylum. Second, Napoleon sought reconciliation with Europe's Catholics, signing, in 1801, a concordat with the pope. In 1804, he enlisted the pope to put a public seal of approval on his reign. Then, on December 1, 1804, Napoleon re-married Josephine in a Catholic ceremony. The next day, with the pope personally overseeing the event, Napoleon crowned himself emperor, and Josephine empress, of the French. Not content with merely a replica of Charlemagne's crown, Napoleon also wore a golden crown shaped like a laurel wreath, an intentional nod to his comparison with Caesar. Third, Napoleon hoped to bring religious peace to the Jews in the lands he influenced. In 1799, then-General Bonaparte "published a proclamation in which he invites all the Jews of Asia and Africa to gather under his flag in order to re-establish the ancient Jerusalem." In 1806, as emperor, Napoleon summoned an Assembly of Jewish Notables. This was followed by The Grand Sanhedrin in 1807. Next, in 1808, Napoleon issued a decree that, among other things, called for the erection of a synagogue in every French department or group of departments with 2,000 Jews. A decade later, in 1816, Napoleon explained his policies of toleration of Jews:

> My primary desire was to liberate the Jews and make them full citizens. I wanted to confer upon them all the legal rights of equality, liberty and fraternity as was enjoyed by the Catholics and Protestants. It is my wish that the Jews be treated like brothers as if we were all part of Judaism. As an added benefit, I thought that this would bring to France many riches because the Jews are numerous and they would come in large numbers to our country where they would enjoy more privileges than in any other nation. Without the

> events of 1814, most of the Jews of Europe would have come to France where equality, fraternity and liberty awaited them and where they can serve the country like everyone else.

As the above quotation from 1816 suggests, Napoleon not only envisioned Jews and Catholics as full citizens of France, but also Protestants. His actual policies when First Consul in 1802 reflect this desire. For it was in 1802 that a law known as the Organic Articles did for Protestants what the Concordat of 1801 did for Catholics. These religious reforms were just some of the many revolutionary and later imperial changes Napoleon enacted for the people of France.

Period ivory Plaques by Noël of Napoleon and Josephine after the coronation.

His new administration occasionally even employed plebiscites, referendums, or direct consultations with the people, who were asked to say yes or no to a specific proposal. In December 1799, for example, Frenchmen voted to establish the Consulate. In May 1802, they voted to establish the Consulate for life. Two years later, they voted to install the Empire. With the people behind him, Napoleon continued to found new institutions to benefit his subjects. In 1800, after reorganizing the old royal provinces, he created the office of Préfet as the executive head for each new department. That same year, he established a new currency by creating the Banque de France to centralize and stabilize banking and to mint money. New schools included "écoles populaires," elementary schools run by the local municipalities, as well as "instituts," independent schools equivalent to "collèges," which were municipal communal secondary schools. The collèges ranked a bit lower than "lycées," special state-run secondary schools for boys with a military flavor, set up in 1802. In the lycées, students wore military uniforms and drum rolls signaled the beginning and end of classes. New incentives to motivate the French included the 1802 establishment of The Legion of Honor, composed of "chevaliers" or knights. The new Civil Code, or as it came to be known after 1808, the Code Napoleon, was issued in 1804. It was the first comprehensive codification of French law, which included legislation on divorce.

These reforms, undertaken from 1799 to 1804, transformed France from a republic to an empire; however, they did not enjoy universal acclaim. Among Napoleon's critics were the French writer Madame Anne-Louise-Germaine Necker de Staël-Holstein and the German composer Ludwig van Beethoven, who originally intended to dedicate his 1804 "Eroica" symphony to Napoleon. The dedication ultimately went to Prince Joseph Franz Maximilian Lobkowitz. Beethoven was apparently in agreement with Napoleon playing the role of a consul, but opposed him elevating himself to emperor. Indeed, once again Napoleon went from imitating one of his heroes to emulating another one. In this case, he would swap Caesar for Charlemagne.

As 1804 ended, Napoleon faced new international pressure as the Third Coalition of nations allied against France took shape. England had declared war on France in May 1803 and was joined by Sweden in 1804, with the addition of Russia and Austria imminent. The year 1805 loomed menacingly to France and its emperor.

5. Napoleon as Charlemagne (1804-1807)

The uneasy peace the Napoleonic Caesar achieved to conclude the French Revolutionary Wars did not last long. The Third Coalition against France's new Charlemagne began another phase in the international conflict that some, but not all, historians refer to as the Napoleonic Wars. Amid this new conflict, on March 17, 1805, Napoleon and Josephine became king and queen of Italy, the crowning taking place at the Cathedral of Milan. Now an empress and a queen, Josephine lived extravagantly, flaunting her many jewels and exotic pets, including two black swans from Western Australia and a dog named Fortuné. Yet, despite the splendor, she was charitable and earned the nickname "the Good Josephine." At this point, Napoleon and his empress were certainly the toast of France.

Nevertheless, their fellow European monarchs still did not accept them as legitimate rulers, even though the French electorate had given Napoleon a 99 percent vote of approval to assume the throne in May 1804. Britain chafed at having to give up the territories it had seized since 1793, and Napoleon was livid that Britain would not turn over Malta. Perhaps sensing the coming struggle with his neighbors, Napoleon deftly promoted 18 of his generals to the rank of marshal of the empire, a move correctly calculated to ensure their loyalty, at least for the immediate future.

19th-century porcelain plaque showing the Battle of Austerlitz.

Thus, Napoleon, now emperor of the French and king of Italy, faced another array of enemies. The Third Coalition consisted of France's perennial enemies Britain and Austria, joined by Sweden, Russia, The Holy Roman Empire, Naples, Sicily, and the remaining exiled French Royalists. Among Napoleon's allies were Spain, Bavaria, Württemberg, Polish Legions, and those portions of Italy that France controlled. Britain had already declared war on France in 1803, and in turn, Napoleon again planned to invade Britain. Looming war with another British-led coalition and the debacle in Haiti had led to the sale of the Louisiana Territory to the United States in 1803, with money from the sale going to fund Napoleon's rearmament. One of history's greatest military leaders, Napoleon best demonstrated his genius when he faced the combined armies of Austria and Russia in a series of battles that culminated at Austerlitz. That huge confrontation, on December 2, 1805, has been called the "Battle of Three Emperors," with Napoleon standing against Alexander I of Russia and Francis II of Austria. Napoleon's *Grande Armée* met a combined force of Russian and Austrian troops near the tiny Moravian village of Austerlitz, Where 67,000 French battled against 85,400 in the Austrian and Russian armies. Ultimately, France suffered 9,000 dead, wounded, or captured versus 36,000 casualties for its enemies.

Period bronze medallion showing Charlemagne and Napoleon.

Napoleon's defeat of the united Russian and Austrian forces at Austerlitz endures as a tactical masterpiece ranking with Alexander the Great's victory at Arbela in 331 BC, Hannibal's triumph at Cannae in 216 BC, and Frederick the Great's victory at Leuthen in 1757, and of course, Charlemagne's many campaigns as that great king conquered his way across Europe. Napoleon's greatest victory effectively destroyed the Third Coalition. It also led to the eventual dissolution of the Holy Roman Empire in 1806, more than 1,000 years after it was founded by Charlemagne on Christmas Day in 800. Napoleon's 1805 campaign also cemented his status as a military overlord of both western and central Europe. The peace agreements that concluded this war began the transformation of a disunited European continent into a unified Napoleonic *Grande Empire*. With France extending its domination into western and southern Germany, Napoleon changed the political face of Europe, but he was not done yet. Nor did he limit his ambitions to Europe only.

Although Austria had been neutralized for the next four years, Britain and Russia remained unvanquished, casting over Napoleon's empire an ominous shadow that had to be addressed. Bonaparte had amassed a French invasion force at Boulogne that trained and prepared for the invasion of Britain that never came. It was the sea, Napoleon's great nemesis, that would prevent this planned attack from happening. He would have to defeat the British navy before Great Britain could be successfully invaded. For the naval Battle of Trafalgar on October 21, 1805, between 33 French and allied ships of the line and 27 British ships of the line seemed to be a good bet for Napoleon to win supremacy of the seas. In fact, it was a debacle for the French navy that forever precluded an invasion of Britain. Ten of the French ships were captured, another sunk, and their Spanish ally lost 11 ships captured. The French and their allies lost over 13,000 men, while the British lost only 1,666. Despite Napoleon's seeming numerical advantage, many capable French naval officers had been executed or purged during the Revolution, and British naval gunnery was so superior that mere numbers of ships and guns did little to indicate an advantage. Trafalgar occurred as Napoleon was leading his army to a great victory on land. At the Battle of Ulm, French troops killed or captured three-quarters of an Austrian army of 40,000 men, with the French losing only 500 dead and 1,000 wounded. Communications being what they were at the time, it would be several weeks before Napoleon heard of the disaster at Trafalgar.

To strike at Britain and Russia, Napoleon contemplated forming some kind of alliance with an Asian Islamic empire, either the Ottoman Turks or the Persians. Such prospects seemed a real possibility in the early months of 1806. In February of that year, Ottoman Sultan Selim III recognized Napoleon as emperor and even called France "our sincere and natural ally." This alliance produced mixed results for the Turks. From 1807 to 1809, the Ottomans managed to defeat the British in an Anglo-Turkish War. They did not prevail, however, in the parallel Russo-Turkish War, which lasted from 1806 to 1812. Meanwhile, Napoleon also formed a Franco-Persian alliance, but it collapsed in 1807.

While stirring up conflicts in the Middle East, Napoleon's successes in continental Europe continued in the 1806 to 1807 War of the Fourth Coalition and its immediate aftermath. In this conflict, Prussia, rather than Austria, would serve as Napoleonic France's major German opponent. Prussian motives for joining this new coalition stemmed in part from Napoleon's establishment of the Confederation of the Rhine in 1806. He intended this collection of German states to serve as a buffer between France and central Europe. Nevertheless, France's reorganization of German territory threatened Prussian influence in Europe's fragmented German-speaking lands. Support for war with France rose steadily in Berlin throughout the summer of 1806, especially from the beautiful and determined Prussian Queen Louise, and Prussia's King Frederick William III ultimately decided to challenge France's attempt to dominate central Europe.

This decision proved disastrous for Prussia. In a sort of blitzkrieg, Napoleon invaded Prussia with 180,000 troops. At the twin battles of Jena and Auerstedt on October 14, 1806, the French crushingly defeated the Prussians, inflicting heavy casualties. The French lost only 6,830 dead and wounded to Prussian losses of 38,000 dead, wounded, and captured. France achieved this feat while badly outnumbered, fielding only 67,000 men against Prussian forces numbering 120,500. Such a lopsided victory had momentous consequences on the morale of the survivors on both sides. As the historian David Chandler wrote in his 1966 book *The Campaigns of Napoleon* of the Prussian forces, "Never has the morale of any army been more completely shattered." Nevertheless, despite having endured an overwhelming defeat, the Prussians refused to negotiate with the French, at least not until the Russians had an opportunity to enter the fight. Never mind what happened just a year prior when Russia fought alongside Austria at Austerlitz.

Napoleon followed up his victory by beginning a trade blockade against Britain, known as the Continental System. The Berlin Decree issued in November 1806 prohibited all the European nations under Napoleon's thumb from trading with Britain. Over the next few months, Napoleon marched against the Russian armies advancing through Poland. In this at times precarious campaign, the French did not always seem likely to prevail. In early February 1807, for instance, Napoleon fought the forces of both Prussia and Russia to a bloody stalemate known as the Battle of Eylau. Both sides suffered losses numbering perhaps in the tens of thousands. Tactically the battle was a French victory, but strategically it was inconclusive. Thus, the war continued. On June 10, 1807, yet another indecisive battle was fought at Heilsberg, this time with the Russo-Prussians winning a tactical victory but France retaining the strategic advantage. The situation finally reached a decisive conclusion on June 14. At the Battle of Friedland, the French practically annihilated the Russian army. Of a force estimated at 46,000 to 62,000 men, the Russians lost an appalling 20,000 killed, wounded, and captured. French losses were considerably smaller, as few as 8,000 to as many as 12,000. The horrifying scale of Russia's defeat convinced Tsar Alexander I of Russia that he had to make peace with the French.

Period burl wood snuffbox with a gold medallion showing Napoleon and Alexander embracing at Tilsit, while the King Frederick William III of Prussia looks on.

Just a few days later, on June 19, the Tsar asked for an armistice. Napoleon decided the Vistula River would represent the natural borders between French and Russian influence in Europe. The two emperors met on a raft on the River Niemen between Russia and East Prussia and negotiated peace at the town of Tilsit. The first thing Alexander said to Napoleon was something that assuredly pleased the latter immensely: "I hate the English as much as you do." Perhaps seeing a kindred spirit in at least their shared loathing of the British, or perhaps not being as power-hungry as he has sometimes been portrayed, Napoleon offered his Russian counterpart relatively lenient peace terms. Russia was to join the Continental System, withdraw its forces from Wallachia and Moldavia on the frontiers of Romania, and give the Ionian Islands on Greece's western coast to France.

Napoleon was not so forgiving with Prussia. Queen Louise, who had ranked among the militaristic faction that favored war with France, came to Napoleon amid the peace negotiations. In a dramatic scene, she even threw herself at his feet, begging him for a better settlement. Her theatrics failed. By the terms of the peace treaty with this now humbled German state, Prussia lost roughly half of its territory, which unintentionally fomented Prussian, if not broader German, nationalist opposition to Napoleon for the remainder of his reign. Nevertheless, for all intents and purposes, Prussia seemed effectively neutered, and Russia emerged as a powerful new friend to Napoleonic France.

Such appearances were deceiving. Russia would not be the steadfast friend Napoleon had hoped for, but that empire had not yet violated its treaty with France. At least at the time of the Treaties of Tilsit, it seemed that Napoleon had gained a great ally with whom he could collaborate on various schemes to change the world. Another factor gave credence to this optimistic view of French prospects. During this conflict, Europeans witnessed, and in some cases participated in, various collaborative ventures with Napoleonic rule that can be characterized as Napoleon's "Spoils System."

Perhaps most important among Napoleon's collaborators were his often unreliable family members. Napoleon rewarded his relatives, and himself, with thrones of their own in 1806, amid the final collapse of Charlemagne's 1,000-year empire. Caroline Bonaparte Murat became Duchess of Guastalla but reigned only a single year; Joseph-Napoleon Bonaparte became king of Naples for two years; Louis Napoleon Bonaparte became king of Holland, holding that throne until 1810; Napoleon himself was protector of the Confederation of the Rhine until 1813; and Jérôme-Napoleon

Bonaparte became king of Westphalia from 1807 to 1813. Finally, Elisa Bonaparte Baciocchi, already princess of Lucca and Piombino since 1805, became grand duchess of Tuscany, holding both titles until her brother's fall from power in 1814.

Around the same time, Napoleon expanded his economic warfare against his British foes, the one European enemy he seemed incapable of defeating. His Continental System, which now included Russia and all those territories he and his siblings ruled, was an attempt to starve Britain by closing European ports to British trade.

While ruling the European continent, Napoleon sponsored public works to improve the French Empire's infrastructure. With the bee as Napoleon's emblem of industry, he also sought to showcase his imperial grandeur. Among the monuments to his glory were various arches of triumph that still stand today. Paris's massive Arc de Triomphe de l'Étoile was begun in 1806 but not completed until 1832, well after Napoleon's death. Like the smaller but still impressive Arc de Triomphe du Carrousel in the same city, which was finished in 1808, it hearkens back to the days when Roman emperors celebrated their victorious campaigns with such monuments.

By the end of 1806, when work was underway on these triumphal arches, the War of the Third Coalition had ended with France and Austria signing the Treaty of Pressburg. This pact tightened France's grip on the Continent and left Italy largely under Napoleon's empire as well. Of course, in the Napoleonic Era, war was never really over, and within months the War of the Fourth Coalition had begun, to last until June 1807. That latest coalition of Britain, Russia, Prussia, Sweden, and Saxony had sprung from the ashes of the third, after Napoleon's attempts to reach peace agreements with Britain and Russia and an alliance with Prussia all failed. One point of contention was Hanover, a German state France had occupied and ruled since 1803 but which both Prussia and Britain claimed. Hanover was especially important to Britain, being its royal family's ancestral home. Swedish troops sent to "liberate" Hanover during the Third Coalition had been ousted by the French in 1806, giving Sweden a reason to resume the fight. While the Prussians previously had tried to stay out of the war with France, creation of the Confederation of the Rhine angered them enough to join in the Fourth Coalition.

The *Grande Armée*'s stunning success at Jena and Auerstedt had crushed the Prussians just 19 days into the war. That, and Napoleon's treaty with Russia, left only Sweden and Britain as viable enemies, but Sweden soon agreed to peace with France, too. The Swedes did retain enough independence to stay out of Napoleon's Continental System. Having eliminated threats from his continental enemies, Napoleon was ready to attempt economic warfare against the only holdout, Great Britain. The Continental System was in force by November 1806, essentially forbidding countries on the Continent to trade with Britain. If Napoleon could not invade Britain, perhaps he could strangle the island economically. Also that autumn, the Treaty of Fontainebleau had made Spain an official ally of France, permitting free passage of French troops through Spain in return for Napoleon allowing Spain to annex Portugal. The French Empire and Napoleon Bonaparte were at their collective zenith, and all seemed well for l'empereur. Napoleon's military successes on the European continent from 1805 to 1807 ushered in a roughly five-year period of imperial glory, which would be marred only by Napoleon's inability to stay out of internal Spanish royal intrigues.

The failure to defeat Britain at sea and to coerce the Russians into a true alliance or cooperative partnership laid the seeds of problems yet to sprout, the foundations of what would become Napoleon's undoing.

Napoleon's comparison to Charlemagne goes only so far, as each of these emperors had a very different ending. Charlemagne would die in Aachen, the seat of the Holy Roman Empire, at the age of 71, still reigning and with his son and heir already crowned. Napoleon would die in exile at the premature age of 51, with no heir and no empire left, far from his beloved country and without family to comfort him.

In 1807, however, such a divergent fate between himself and his idol was not what Napoleon would have predicted.

6. Imperial Glory (1807-1812)

During the height of Napoleon's power, he faced one of his biggest challenges: The Peninsular War and the Fifth Coalition of 1807 through 1809. Despite having secured peace with Russia and Prussia at Tilsit, Napoleon now had to organize his expanded empire and enforce the Continental System against the British. To do so, he focused his attention on reining in the Kingdom of Portugal. The Portuguese had violated his trade prohibitions and were doing business with Britain. After the French and Spanish navies had been defeated at Trafalgar in 1805, Portugal's future King John VI the Clement, who was prince regent due to his mentally ill mother, had agreed to close his ports to British trade. Nevertheless, in defiance of Napoleon's orders, John soon resumed not only diplomatic relations, but also trade with Britain.

Highly displeased, Napoleon followed up his victory over Russia and Prussia by sending an army to invade Portugal. On October 17, 1807, General Jean-Andoche Junot led 24,000 French troops across the Pyrenees into Spanish territory. Spain permitted this army to traverse its lands toward its neighbor on the Iberian Peninsula. What became known as the Peninsular War became a drawn-out, six-year affair that bled the French army and diverted valuable troops, attention, and resources from other theaters that may have been more important.

By the winter of 1808, with Napoleonic forces moving throughout the Iberian Peninsula, French agents conducted intrigues in the internal affairs of their Spanish ally. The two main factions in Spain were those who supported King Charles IV versus those who supported Charles's son and eventual successor as King Ferdinand VII. The factions could further be distinguished as those who favored an alliance with France versus those who favored an alliance with the United Kingdom. Charles was then allied with France, whereas supporters of Ferdinand (called "Fernandistas") preferred a British alliance. With apparent discord stoked by French agents dividing members of the Spanish royal family, Napoleon announced on February 16, 1808, that he would intervene as a mediator between Spain's rival factions. The "mediation" included sending French Marshal Murat into Spain with 120,000 troops. This new French force arrived in Madrid on March 24. It was not welcomed. Instead, riots soon erupted against what Spaniards perceived as a foreign occupation. To the further outrage of many, in the summer of 1808 Napoleon appointed his brother, Joseph Bonaparte, as the new king of Spain. The country's devoutly religious and conservative population was outraged at this imposition of a French monarch who had no significant ties to their nation. Especially galling were Joseph's ties to a Masonic Lodge, considered anathema by the Catholic Church. Joseph and his loyal Spanish followers (called "Josefinos" by rebellious Spaniards) were held in contempt by the public. One thing Joseph did accomplish during his reign was finally putting an end to the Spanish Inquisition. That did little to quell the discontent. Throughout Spain, resistance to French occupation spread to such an extent that in July, the French suffered a major defeat at the Battle of Bailén. Spanish casualties and losses numbered a mere 243 dead and 735 wounded versus French losses of some 2,200 dead, 400 wounded, and 17,635 captured. After retreating to the north, Joseph asked Napoleon's permission to abdicate, but his imperial brother would hear none of his defeatism. Instead, Napoleon sent reinforcements. To stave off total disaster, the French emperor decided to intervene in person, and promptly recaptured Madrid. This action served to prove that Joseph's command of French forces on the peninsula was an illusion. Before taking action, French generals would consult Napoleon and not Joseph. Among other calamities during Joseph's reign, Spain's colonial empire began to crumble. Venezuela, in 1810, was the first Spanish colony to declare its independence. Joseph eventually abdicated in 1813.

Before entering his personal Iberian adventure, Napoleon had to make sure he would not find himself facing a two-front war.

The danger was that with Napoleon busy in Spain and Portugal, Russia or Austria might be tempted to seize the chance to violate their agreements with France reached at Tilsit in 1807. So before going on a campaign across the Pyrenees, Napoleon took time for some diplomatic fence-mending. In October 1808, at the Congress of Erfurt, he addressed various lingering issues with the Russians. Both France and Russia would agree to the terms of the Erfurt Convention, including a demand that Britain conclude its war against France, French recognition of Russia's conquest of Finland from Sweden, and Russian affirmation of support for France in a possible war against Austria. Having thus restored and clarified his alliance with Russia, Napoleon returned to France and prepared for war in Spain.

Napoleon personally commanded the *Grande Armée* in its rapid crossing of the Ebro River in November 1808. He achieved much greater success than his subordinates had the previous year. On November 30, he defeated the Spanish at the Battle of Somosierra. The French only lost 57 dead or wounded; the Spanish toll was 250 dead or wounded, and another 3,000 captured. On December 3, Napoleon entered Madrid with 80,000 troops and then set his soldiers against British forces that by then were aiding the Spanish resistance. In just over a month, the French drove the British all the way to the coast. After the last stand at the Battle of Corunna on January 16, 1809, in which their commander was mortally wounded, the British withdrew from Spain, leaving behind just a few hundred of their sick.

A Spanish paper mâché transfer print snuffbox showing Lord Wellington during the Peninsular campaign.

For the time being, Napoleon was triumphant in Spain, but soon had to leave Iberia to deal with a renewed Austrian threat in Central Europe. In his absence, the Peninsular War continued, but Napoleon would never return to Spain. Several months after Corunna, Britain sent yet another army to the peninsula, this time led by the future Duke of Wellington. The war settled into a complex and asymmetric strategic struggle highlighted by brutal guerrilla warfare. That irregular combat–the term "guerrilla" originated in this campaign–brought terror to much of Spain's countryside. The Spanish guerrillas tied down an enormous number of the 300,000

French troops on the peninsula, who were relegated to protecting supply lines and static locations. Napoleon and the French had not experienced this sort of popular national uprising in other European nations. The strain of such fighting, where every civilian seemed to be an enemy, resulted in brutality the French Army had not previously encountered or practiced. The horrifying atrocities committed by both sides are perhaps rivaled only by what occurred in Haiti during the Napoleonic Wars. They severely tarnished the reputation and morale of Napoleon's *Grande Armée*.

As Napoleon's forces attempted to suppress resistance in Spain, the *Grande Armée* in 1808 consisted of 350,280 infantry (113 line and 32 light regiments, including 417 battalions), 48,000 cavalries (80 regiments of 320 squadrons), and 1,000 cannons. Of these numbers, some 100,000 of his best troops would go to Spain to join 120,000 "second line" soldiers already there. The vast majority of this massive army was tied down to garrison duty and intelligence operations. Moreover, these forces in Spain shrank by 5,000 men each month, victims of the vicious guerrilla fighting that engulfed the nation and severely disrupted French lines of supply and communication. Obliged to counter widespread harassing attacks, the French remained scattered, unable to concentrate their forces effectively or to apply mass at crucial times and places. It was a critical failure to obey an essential principle of war. Thus, the war in Spain dragged on with no obvious end in sight.

Meanwhile, in central Europe, after four years of relative peace, Austria sought another rematch with France to avenge its earlier defeats. Even though Austria had mutual defense agreements with Russia, it could not realistically hope for Russian help. In 1809, the Tsar's armies were busy battling against Britain, Sweden, and the Ottoman Empire. Instead, Austria hoped for support from Frederick William of Prussia, who initially promised to help. Before the conflict began, however, Frederick William reneged. If Austria's hope for allies was not disappointing enough, the Habsburg Archduke Charles even warned that his own empire was not ready for another war with France. Despite these ominous indications that by attacking France Austria would be at serious risk, those in the Austrian government advocating for war won out. On February 8, 1809, the War of the Fifth Coalition began.

On April 10, elements of the Austrian army crossed the Inn River to invade Bavaria. The Austrian attack surprised the French. Napoleon was in Paris when he heard the news. When he finally arrived at Donauwörth on April 17, he discovered the *Grande Armée* in a precarious position, its two wings separated by 75 miles and joined only by a thin cordon of Bavarian troops. After Archduke Charles pressed the French army's left wing and hurled his men toward the III Corps of Marshal Davout, Napoleon realigned his army's axis. Marching his soldiers towards the town of Eckmühl, he scored a convincing victory there on April 21 and 22. It was the turning point of the 1809 Campaign. Austrian losses were 12,000 killed, wounded, or captured, while the French lost half that number–6,000 killed or wounded. The French victory forced Charles to withdraw across the Danube and into Bohemia. On May 13, for the second time in four years, Vienna fell to Napoleon. But the war continued.

Most of the Austrian army had survived the first battles in southern Germany, in effect living to fight another day. That day rapidly approached. By May 17, Charles and the main Austrian army arrived on the Marchfeld, a plain northeast of Vienna, just across the Danube, that often served as a training ground for Austrian troops. Charles hoped to concentrate his forces at the point where Napoleon would attempt to cross the Danube. The archduke kept the bulk of his troops several miles away from the riverbank. The first major French effort to cross occurred on May 21. That day, the two armies struggled for the villages of Aspern and Essling, focal points of the French bridgehead. For the first time in more than a decade, Napoleon was personally defeated on the battlefield.

Part of the reason he lost the Battle of Aspern-Essling was the Austrians' numerical superiority. On May 21, Charles commanded 110,000 soldiers, while Napoleon had only 31,000. By the battle's second day, although reinforcements had boosted French numbers to 70,000, Napoleon remained outnumbered. Despite a ferocious seesaw struggle for the two villages, a sustained Austrian artillery bombardment proved decisive enough to persuade Napoleon to withdraw his forces onto Lobau Island, a defensible position on the Danube. By the time the dust had settled, both sides had inflicted about 23,000 casualties on each other. This first defeat that Napoleon suffered in a major set-piece battle proved to Europeans that the great captain could be beaten on the battlefield. It was an ominous sign of things to come.

Nevertheless, as with Charles after his defeat at Eckmühl, Napoleon was not finished after his setback at Aspern-Essling. He did, however, take more than six weeks to plan and prepare for contingencies before attempting to cross the Danube again. During that time, French forces commanded by Napoleon's subordinates won victories elsewhere: at Sankt Michael on May 25, Stralsund on May 31, Bergisel on five separate dates from April 12 to November 1, Raab on June 14, and Graz from June 24 to 26. It was after these successes in various theaters that the French again crossed the Danube. With more than 180,000 men marching across the Marchfeld toward the Austrians, the crossing took several days, from June 30 to the early days of July. Charles met this massive French force with 150,000 of his own men.

The ensuing battle was the war's decisive event. For two days, on July 5 and 6, Napoleon personally commanded 154,000 Bavarians, Frenchmen, Italians, and Saxons against 158,000 Austrians. The Battle of Wagram was the largest battle of his career until then. To clinch his victory, Napoleon ordered a concentrated central thrust that punctured a hole in the Austrian lines, forcing Charles to retreat. Although Napoleon lost perhaps 25,000 men in the battle, he had, nevertheless, crushed the Austrians. His enemies suffered as many as 40,000 casualties, dead, wounded, or missing. Thus, Napoleon's preeminence in Europe was reaffirmed.

Of course, Austria was not the only member of the coalition against France. Perhaps if its British ally could win a decisive victory elsewhere, maybe all would not be lost. As Austrian forces continued to struggle against the French in the days following the battle of Wagram, the British prepared an expedition to the Kingdom of Holland. Its purpose was both to open a second front and to relieve the French pressure on the Austrians. Nevertheless, by the time the British army landed at Walcheren on July 30, the Austrians had already been defeated, having agreed to an armistice on July 12. The Walcheren Campaign thus came too late. Curiously, it was characterized by little fighting but heavy casualties from sickness. The popularly named "Walcheren Fever"–a combination of malaria, typhus, typhoid, and other diseases–claimed the lives of many of the over 4,000 British troops who died during the expedition. Only 106 of the British casualties died in combat. Both sides suffered thousands of sick soldiers, but it was the British who withdrew in December 1809. Britain's fiasco did at least manage to delay the political settlement.

The War of the Fifth Coalition, like the four that preceded it, once again resulted in a French victory. The victory was substantial enough that aside from the ongoing Peninsular War and France's war with Britain, much of the rest of western and central Europe would not experience any major conflict for the next three years. The Treaty of Schönbrunn, signed on October 14, 1809, was harsher than those that France had imposed on Austria in the earlier coalition wars. The fundamental goal of Austria's negotiators had been to preserve the Habsburg Empire. They succeeded in doing so, but at the expense of significant territories. France took Carinthia, Carniola, and the Adriatic ports. Galicia was given to the Poles, and the Salzburg portion of the Tyrol went to Bavaria. These territorial changes cost Austria over three million subjects, about a fifth of its total population. Nevertheless, Napoleon did not just want to punish Austria. He had another idea about the seemingly recurrent problem of having to battle against that empire.

Gold snuffbox dated 1810 showing Napoleon and Marie Louise after their wedding.

Having fought a two-front war and defeated Austria yet again, Napoleon hoped to prevent this scenario from repeating itself. His new goal for 1809 was to convert Austria from foe to friend. To do so, Napoleon divorced Josephine, mainly because she could not give Napoleon a son of his own. The male heir Napoleon did have, Napoleon Charles Bonaparte, Josephine's grandson, had died in 1807. At dinner on November 30, 1809, Napoleon informed Josephine of his plans. Afterward, Napoleon's secretary reported that he heard Josephine's screams from the next room. With Josephine's ultimate cooperation, the marriage was nullified on the grounds that a parish priest had not attended the 1804 ceremony. That avoided an actual divorce that would have upset the Catholic Church and the Catholic Emperor Francis I of Austria. His focus now on Austria, Napoleon had hopes to cement his recent alliance with Francis using a family connection. To that end, having been turned down in his proposal to marry Tsar Alexander's youngest sister, Anna Pavlovna, Napoleon then married the 18-year-old Archduchess Marie-Louise of Austria on March 11, 1810, a union Napoleon cynically described as "marrying a womb." Josephine went to live at her chateau at Malmaison, west of Paris. Her health declined over the next few years, and she died in 1814 at the age of 50. Soon after Napoleon's new marriage alliance, on August 21, 1810, his former fiancée, Désirée, became crown princess of Sweden by marrying Jean Bernadotte, a 47-year-old French general who had fought under Napoleon at Austerlitz and Wagram before being elected crown prince of Sweden. Désirée was also the sister of Napoleon's eldest brother's wife. Thus, by year's end, the French Clary, Bernadotte, and Bonaparte families were now intermixed with each other and linked further to the Austrian Habsburgs, thereby dominating western and central Europe.

While one would think Napoleon was the preeminent figure of this extensive, interconnected family, not all of its members actually shared that opinion. Clara Tschudi, author of *Napoleon's Mother* (1900), recounts the following incident:

> The power of the Emperor of France, and the high descent of Marie Louise, never for one moment caused Letitia to forget that she was Napoleon's mother, and possessed a clear claim to respect from him and his wife. At a family meeting one day, he stretched out his hand with a movement which seemed to imply that she ought to kiss it, but she pushed it away.
>
> "Am I not your emperor?" he asked.
>
> "Am I not your mother?" she replied, "and are you not first and foremost my son?" Napoleon was silenced and kissed her hand. Marie Louise, who was present,

> observed to her mother-in-law: "Mama! When I was in Vienna I always kissed the hand of the Emperor of Austria."
>
> "The Emperor of Austria is your father, my child!" answered Letitia. "the Emperor of France is my son—that is the difference!"

Of course, Marie Louise would also have the opportunity to be the mother of an emperor.

Top and bottom of a small crystal box from 1811 showing Napoleon and Marie Louise on the top and the King of Rome on the bottom.

On March 20, 1811, Marie Louise gave birth to a baby boy. Napoleon made him his heir apparent, bestowing on the boy the title of King of Rome. A possible future Napoleon II had taken his first breath, but for his son to eventually become an emperor, Napoleon I would have to maintain his empire in the face of mounting challenges. If he succeeded in finally bringing peace to Europe, Napoleon II's future would look quite bright indeed. But if the emperor were to fall from power, his infant son would become little more than a footnote in history.

7. Imperial Decline (1812-1814)

By 1812, Napoleon had consolidated his control of the German and Italian states in western and central Europe, but the Slavic states of eastern Europe remained mostly outside his authority, thanks to Russian refusal to remain part of Napoleon's continental blockade against Britain. Napoleon's attempt to rein in his former Russian allies, known as The Russian Campaign and the War of the Sixth Coalition, began the downfall of France's Grand Empire and its emperor.

Napoleon's spies had alerted him to Tsar Alexander's plans to renege on the Russo-French alliance established at the Congress of Erfurt in 1808. Those plans included an attack on France to regain Poland for the Russians. Relations between the two empires had already been strained by Russia's repeated violations of the Continental System.

In the spring of 1812, Napoleon massed 614,000 men, "an army of twenty nations," on his eastern frontier. Having made extensive but still inadequate logistical preparations, he faced a choice of invasion routes. Napoleon decided that he and his army's main body would advance in three columns along an axis from Smolensk to Moscow. The Prussians would guard the northern flank and the Austrians the southern. Napoleon's inner council urged him not to invade Russia, but he ignored that advice. Indeed, Alexander was aware of Napoleon's plans and had told the French diplomat Armand de Caulaincourt, "Your Frenchman is brave, but long privations and a bad climate wear him down and discourage him. Our climate, our winter, will fight on our side."

Napoleon called this invasion The Second Polish War, attempting to justify the attack by invoking Polish fears of an imminent Russian takeover. His hopes to secure the cooperation of Polish nationalists failed because he would not promise them an independent state.

This lack of commitment resulted, in Polish atrocities against the French during the winter retreat of 1812-1813.

This invasion has far greater importance to Russian popular culture than to the French. Great literary and musical works about The Patriotic War of 1812 abound. For instance, Leo Tolstoy's 1869 novel *War and Peace* is the best-known fictional depiction of that campaign. *The Year 1812* by Pyotr Tchaikovsky, popularly known as the *1812 Overture*, celebrates the Russians' victory over Napoleon's invaders. The memory of this battle remains a potent force in Russian politics. In 2012, the 200th anniversary of Napoleon's failed invasion of Russia, while campaigning for his third term in office, current Russian President Vladimir Putin referred to the Battle of Borodino as symbolic of Russian unity. Later in the year, Putin witnessed thousands of actors reenact the bloody battle. Meanwhile, as part of that same anniversary commemoration, Patriarch Kirill, the head of the Russian Orthodox Church, led a memorial service attended by thousands. What the French experienced 200 years earlier, however, was hardly anything worth celebrating.

In the campaign of 1812, Napoleon and the French advanced, looking for opportunities to do battle with their Russian opponents. The Russians, however, conducted a scorched earth withdrawal, depriving the French of forage from the countryside, an essential element of that era's military campaigns. Napoleon was credited with the remark (even though it may actually have been Frederick the Great who said it) that an army "marches on its stomach." In this case, the stomach was empty. Napoleon entered Vilna on June 28, 1812, and delayed his advance for two weeks. Why? Because as a result of desertion and consequences of the summer heat, his army was already down by a third! Russian Field Marshal Michael Andreas Barclay de Tolly made a brief stand at Smolensk on August 17, then successfully disengaged. A scorched earth policy was fine to a point, but the Tsar was unwilling to let the French take the holy city of Moscow without a fight. The Russians, now under Mikhail

Illarionovich Golenishchev-Kutuzov, made a stand at Borodino on September 7.

In this largest battle of the invasion, Napoleon failed to exploit Kutuzov's open left flank. He resorted to frontal attacks on the Russian redoubts behind a heavy artillery barrage. The French suffered 28,000 casualties and the Russians 52,000. The Russians disengaged during the night and got away clean. Moscow would fall, but Kutuzov had preserved the Russian army as a viable fighting unit.

Napoleon and his *Grand Armée* marched into Moscow expecting the capture of this city to mean an end to hostilities, but they were sadly mistaken. Instead, with their army intact, the Russians had abandoned Moscow and set it ablaze, leaving Napoleon with a burnt-out wreck of a prize and little prospect of feeding his army.

After repeatedly trying to negotiate peace with the Tsar, Napoleon finally abandoned Moscow on October 19, 1812. The *Grande Armée*, now down to 100,000 men, was turned back at Malayaroslavets on the 24th and retreated toward Smolensk. Had Napoleon sent out scouts, he would have discovered that the Russians had withdrawn and a warmer southern route home was possible.

British caricature dated 1812 of 'General Winter' defeating Napoleon during his withdrawal from Russia in 1812.

Falling temperatures eroded the strength of the *Grande Armée* and, with Russian guerrillas on their trail, French soldiers reached Smolensk on November 9. The *Grande Armée* crossed the Berezina

River on November 27-28 with only 60,000 survivors and then ceased to be the *Grande Armée*.

After so much success, how did Napoleon get to this catastrophic point?

The causes of his downfall began first and foremost with his failure to invade Britain. An 1803 English engraving titled *Britannia Correcting an Unruly Boy* is a satire on Britain's fear of French invasion. In this political cartoon, Britannia holds Napoleon across her knee and raises a bundle of birch twigs tied with a ribbon to thrash his bleeding posterior. Britannia says: "There take that and that and that, and be careful not to provoke my Anger more." Napoleon exclaims: "oh forgive me this time and I never will do so again, oh dear! oh dear! You'll entirely spoil the Honors of the Sitting." Placed beside Britannia are her spear and sword; next to Napoleon is his huge hat and saber. The scene is by the sea, with a fleet of retreating vessels flying France's tricolor flag. On the right is a cliff on which a small British lion lies on a scroll inscribed: "Qui uti scit ei bona," meaning "good things to him who knows how to use them." The lion rests atop a cliff overlooking the Channel. Ultimately, this metaphorical spanking of Napoleon by Britannia may have been more consequential to the long-term prospects of Emperor Napoleon's career than the one his mother gave him while he was a youngster.

Just two years after this cartoon was published, British naval forces under Nelson destroyed the combined French and Spanish fleets. The decisive battle of Trafalgar secured England's sea power for the remainder of the era, confining Napoleon's empire to continental Europe only.

Napoleon's inability to conquer Britain caused him to close European ports to British trade. Not surprisingly, not all of Europe was enthusiastic about damaging their economic opportunities in the service of Napoleon's imperial ambitions. To stop such opposition in the Iberian Peninsula, Napoleon sent in his armies again. There he faced opposition not just to his economic policies, but also to the French invaders' alleged atheism.

Officially, Napoleon ruled as a Catholic as evidenced by the Imperial Catechism of April 4, 1807, which can be found at http://www.napoleon-series.org/research/government/legislation/c_education.html and is excerpted here:

> Question: What are the duties of Christians with respect to the princes who govern them, and what in particular are our duties towards Napoleon I, our Emperor?
>
> Answer: Christians owe to the princes who govern them, and we owe in particular to Napoleon I, our Emperor, love, respect, obedience, fidelity, military service and the tributes laid for the preservation and defense of the Empire and of his throne; we also owe to him fervent prayers for his safety and the spiritual and temporal prosperity of the State.
>
> Question: Why are we bound to all these duties towards our Emperor?
>
> Answer: First of all, because God, who creates empires and distributes them according to His will, in loading our Emperor with gifts, both in peace and in war, has established him as our sovereign and has made him the minister of His power and His image upon the earth. To honor and to serve our Emperor is then to honor and to serve God himself. Secondly, because our Lord Jesus Christ by his doctrine as well as by His example, has Himself taught us what we owe to our sovereign: He was born the subject of Caesar Augustus; He paid the prescribed impost; and just as He ordered to render to God that which belongs to God, so He ordered to render to Caesar that which belongs to Caesar.
>
> Question: Are there not particular reasons which ought to attach us more strongly to Napoleon I, our Emperor?
>
> Answer: Yes; for it is he whom God has raised up under difficult circumstances to re-establish the public worship of the holy religion of our fathers and to be the protector of it. He has restored and preserved public order by his profound and active wisdom; he defends the State by his powerful

arm; he has become the anointed of the Lord through the consecration which he received from the sovereign pontiff, Head of the Universal Church.

Question: What ought to be thought of those who may be lacking in their duty towards our Emperor?

Answer: According to the Apostle Saint Paul, they would be resisting the order established by God himself and would render themselves worthy of eternal damnation.

The Spanish did not share this vision of divine support for Napoleon's rule. Instead, they responded with a particularly fascinating bit of anti-French propaganda within the question-and-answer framework of a catechism. This example shows both the motives for Spanish resistance to the French and the nature of anti-French resistance:

Question: How is this child named?

Response: As a Spaniard.

Q: What is a Spaniard?

R: An honest man.

Q: How many duties does he have and what are they?

R: Three. To be a Christian of the Roman Catholic faith, to defend his religion, his King and his country, and to die rather than be conquered.

Q: Who is our King?

R: Ferdinand VII.

Q: With how much love should he be honored?

R: With the greatest love, as his virtues and misfortunes have merited.

Q: Who is the enemy of our happiness?

R: The Emperor of the French.

Q: Who is he?

R: A new and infinitely evil ruler, a greedy chief of all evil men and the exterminator of the good, the essence and receptacle of every vice.

Q: How many natural forms does he assume?

R: Two. One a devil and the other human.
Q: How many Emperors are there?
R: There is one true Emperor, with three false faces.
Q: What are they?
R: Napoleon, Murat and Godoy.
Q: What are the characteristics of the first of these?
R: Arrogance and tyranny.
Q: And of the second?
R: Plunder and cruelty.
Q: And of the last?
R: Treason and disgrace.
Q: Who are the French?
R: Old Christians and modern heretics.
Q: What has brought them to this state?
R: False philosophy, and placing liberty above old customs.
Q: How do they serve their ruler?
R: Some feed his arrogance, and others are agents of his iniquity in the extermination of the human race.

The propaganda war conducted during the quagmire in Spain coincided with that drawn-out war's atrocities. For example, in August 1810 at Villafranca, the men of the guerrilla leader Juan Martin Diez inflicted horrific punishments on French prisoners and Spaniards accused of collaboration with the invaders. Historian John Lawrence Tone described this guerrilla campaign:

> A guerrilla band, possibly a detachment from the Emperinado's party, entered Villafranca in August 1810, during the period when Mina was still far from having established his ascendancy in Navarre after the capture of Javier. The guerrillas captured five of the fifteen grenadiers stationed in the town along with a local woman who had made the mistake of marrying one of the French soldiers. The woman was stripped, tarred, and beaten as she was led, mounted backward on a mule, through the town with a notice attached to her back reading "whore of the French."

> On the following day, she was placed in a wooden cage in the town square to witness the death of the five grenadiers. The unlucky captives were buried alive with only their heads above the ground, while the Spanish troops took turns trying to hit their heads with a large wooden ball. When the last "goal" had ceased to cry out, the game was over. The poor woman, after having one of her ears cut off—a torture commonly practiced by both sides—was carted to Puente la Reina, where she was nailed to the church door until she bled to death. Two years of seeing men shot, hanged, and impaled in roadside trees had led to a complete breakdown of ethical norms of conduct. And the terror was to become much worse and more systematic before things improved.

Tragically, the atrocities at Villafranca were among many such horrors that occurred during the Peninsular War.

In some of the other equally shocking incidents, men and women actually had their sex organs butchered. As described by Captain Charles-François François, officers, soldiers, even women were mutilated:

> slit open from uterus to stomach, with breasts cut off. Men were sawn in half, others' penises had been cut off and placed in their mouths; others were buried alive up to their shoulders with their genitals in their mouth, and others were hung by their feet inside of chimneys, their heads consumed by fire. 53 men were buried up to their shoulders. 400 men had had their throats slit, were cut into pieces, and cast into the streets and yards. Brave General René was cut in half in front of his wife, after having watched her being raped; then their child was cut in half before its mother, who was finally murdered in the same manner. We found the bodies of our soldiers, whose noses, ears, limbs, and tongues had been cut off, and others whose fingernails and eyes had been torn out. A French officer, after having had his eyelids and fingernails removed, was cut into pieces and fed

to pigs; the healthier soldiers were stoned, cut into pieces, and strewn in the road. Some Spaniards said these crimes were inspired by the priests' advice to the inhabitants.

Of course, atrocities were not limited to this campaign or to peasants. But peasants did seem to have engaged in more than their share. The noted scholar Adam Zamoyski related some similar atrocities during the Russian campaign.

The Russians were no less brutal. Most of the prisoners were taken by Cossacks, whose first action was invariably to strip them and take not only all valuables but also all serviceable items of clothing. They would then hand them over, or preferably sell them, to local peasants, who would massacre them with varying degrees of sadism.

Some would be buried alive, and others would be tied to trees and used for target practice, others would have their ears, noses, tongues, and genitalia cut off, and so on. General Wilson saw "sixty dying naked men, whose necks were laid upon a felled tree, while Russian men and women, with large faggot-sticks, singing in chorus and hopping around, with repeated blows struck out their brains in succession." At Dorogobuzh, Woldermar von Löenstern was horrified to see Russian troops stand by while the locals massacred unarmed camp followers with axes, pitchforks, and clubs. "It was a ghastly spectacle," he wrote, "they looked like cannibals and a fierce joy lit up their faces."

After Waterloo, the Austrians and Prussians were noted for their violence against the Belgian and French populace, "roaring, drinking, pillaging, ransacking, and raping, with utter disregard as to who was on which side. Entire cities were sacked, and what soldiers could not take with them, they destroyed, including farmer's crops in the fields."

There is no question that soldiers on all sides, French and Allied, committed their share of atrocities, especially rape and pillage. Such horrors have, sadly, been part of wars for as long as such conflicts have existed, but cruelty inflicted by peasants was generally far more brutal, especially when it came to sexual torture. For one thing, they generally did not have officers trying to keep them under control, and revenge was often a factor. In the case of the Spanish, they had a history of such actions in the form of the Inquisition, which Napoleon ended when he came to Spain. There is ample evidence that Spanish priests often encouraged the worst behavior toward the French and their sympathizers, though there is also proof that priests and city officials sometimes intervened on behalf of the victims.

Perhaps even bloodier than these massacres were the Spanish quagmire's many sieges and battles. The French won some key victories in their attempt to retake Portugal by way of Spain. These "victories" included successes at the siege of Ciudad Rodrigo from April through July 1810, at the cost of 180 killed and over 1,000 wounded, and then at the siege of Almeida in July and August 1810, with losses of 58 dead and 320 wounded. Nevertheless, the French were next defeated at the battle of Buçaco on September 27, 1810, in which they lost 4,500 dead or wounded. With the tide turning in Portugal, a British force under Sir Arthur Wellesley, Duke of Wellington, held off Napoleonic troops for seven months in 1810 and 1811 at the siege of Torres Vedras. The French lost again at the battle of Sabugal on April 3, 1811, and the battle of Fuentes de Oñoro from May 3 to 5, 1811, sustaining combined casualties for these two battles of some 4,384 killed, wounded, or captured. After the French were permanently expelled from Portugal, their terrifying losses continued in Spain. During the 1812 battle of Salamanca, 51,949 British and Portuguese under Wellington decisively defeated 49,646 French troops in Spain. Britain and Portugal suffered 5,167 dead or wounded, versus 6,000 French dead or wounded. Another 7,000 French were captured.

While these battles raged in Spain, Napoleon's forces were suffering even more horrendous losses as they retreated from Russia.

Hand-painted German snuffbox from 1813 or 1814 showing a caricature of Napoleon as a nutcracker standing on a coffin unable to crack the nut of Leipzig. Note his broken teeth on the lid of the coffin.

In 1813, after the French and Russians somewhat recovered from the previous year's campaign, the War of the Sixth Coalition began. Initially, Napoleon won all battles, but a war of attrition worked against the French. At the battle of Leipzig, from October 16 through 19, allied forces claimed an overwhelming victory against Napoleon. This "Battle of the Nations" marked the end of French rule in Germany. A frequently reproduced German caricature of Napoleon was created in late 1813 to mark the major defeat of his forces at Leipzig. In that massive battle, France lost an almost incomprehensible 38,000 dead and wounded and 20,000 captured.

The Coalition allies offered France peace by way of the Frankfurt Proposals, which would allow Napoleon to remain Emperor but require France to retreat to her "natural frontiers." In perhaps the worst mistake of his life, Napoleon refused, despite being warned that the offer would only get harsher as time went on. The war continued. To be fair, Napoleon might have suffered serious political problems at home had he agreed to essentially negate all that France had gained, at great cost, during his reign. Besides, ever the optimist, Napoleon assumed that France–meaning himself–would win this war as he had won all the other wars of the coalitions. But as his fortunes declined after a series of defeats, the Allies were good to their word, and refused to repeat the original proposal. Instead, The British insisted on removing Napoleon from power.

Now grossly outnumbered by at least three to one, the French army could not hope to win the war. The French Senate defied their emperor and on April 1, 1814, voted to surrender. That vote was for what they called "The Emperor's Demise Act" (*Acte de déchéance de l'Empereur*), which declared Napoleon deposed. Napoleon's generals refused to march on Paris, and he was left with no choice but to abdicate, which he did on April 4, 1814, in favor of his son, Napoleon II. The Allies refused this obvious attempt at somehow retaining power, and two days later Napoleon abdicated for real. Now at the mercy of the Allies, he faced exile on Elba.

After Napoleon's 1814 abdication, Tsar Alexander I stepped in to protect Josephine. The Russian emperor guaranteed that she would not suffer the same bloody fate as France's previous monarchic consort, Queen Marie Antoinette, who was guillotined in 1793. Instead, Josephine died of natural causes on May 29, 1814, at Malmaison, the country home she had shared with Napoleon. Her death came not long after a walk in Malmaison's gardens with her Russian protector. Her last words, however, were not about Alexander but "Bonaparte . . . the island of Elba . . . the King of Rome."

When the defeated and exiled Napoleon learned of Josephine's death, he locked himself in a room for two days. He was in exile on a Mediterranean island, had suffered the catastrophic losses of hundreds of thousands of his soldiers, no longer ruled an empire, and now would never again see the greatest love of his life. For any normal man, recovering from such a fall might be unimaginable. But Napoleon was not any normal man.

8. Napoleon's Return and Last Stand (1814-1815)

After his generals' lack of commitment forced Napoleon's abdication, the Great Man was exiled to the island of Elba, but the victorious allies, led by the British, granted him more power and access than would prove prudent. Elba being so close to Bonaparte's ancestral homeland of Corsica and in such proximity to mainland Europe, sending the ambitious ex-emperor into exile there could be compared to dangling a carrot in front of a horse's nose. It is only natural that thoughts and schemes of a return to power would flourish in such an environment. Napoleon had been allowed to retain his title of emperor, and had a small army and navy at his disposal. That army numbered around 700 men, though it was supposedly limited by treaty to only 400. With his title and his fighting forces, and being in full command of the island, Napoleon did not feel totally defeated. Would not the emperor of a great nation want to return to his seat of power and resume his rule? It seems logical and obvious to us in retrospect, a point the allies apparently missed. Perhaps this mistake was on the minds of another set of allies a century later when the Treaty of Versailles was drafted. Its intention was to ensure that Germany knew unequivocally who had won and who had lost World War I.

A very large period engraving showing Napoleon's triumphal return at the start of the 100 Days.

The 21 articles of the Treaty of Fontainebleau allowed Napoleon to keep his title of emperor and Marie-Louise hers as empress, and let him rule Elba, an island of about 12,000 people, as if it were his own. The treaty forbade Napoleon's relatives and heirs from attaining power in France. Marie-Louise was permitted to remain Duchess of Parma, Duchess of Placentia, and Duchess of Guastalla, and her male heir would become prince of those places. The former Empress Josephine was not treated so well; her allowance was cut from 3 million francs to a million francs annually. Of course, Napoleon was forced to cede his other lands and estates, and was ordered to return all crown jewels. Although signed by representatives of Austria, Russia, Prussia, and France, the English refused to sign the treaty on the grounds that doing so would legitimize Napoleon's reign. According to Britain's interpretation, France was a country in the midst of rebellion, with Napoleon the usurper of the legitimate Bourbon government.

Allowed free access to newspapers and letters, Napoleon was kept well informed of world events despite the watchfulness of his Austrian and French royalist guards. Working hard to improve the island, Bonaparte may have seemed happy to be the administrator of a small place, but instead of being content to rule Elba, he never ceased the intrigues, plotting a return to power. Napoleon also suffered the indignity of not receiving his agreed-upon annual allowance of 2 million francs. He feared rumors that he was to be moved to a far more remote location where he would live under harsher circumstances. Possibilities for this more distant exile that he heard included Fort George in Scotland, a floating prison hulk in England, or the remote mid-Atlantic island of St. Helena. Napoleon was also painfully aware of the decline of France's fortunes in world affairs, with the Empire shrinking and unrest wracking the nation. He also shrewdly observed from a distance the tensions among those nations that had defeated him, tensions that seemed to presage war among his adversaries. From November 1814 through June 1815, at the Congress of Vienna, these former allied nations bickered and postured and threatened war to achieve their claims, while redrawing the map of Europe.

When French soldiers who had become prisoners of war returned home, Napoleon knew he could find a large and ready source of veteran troops for a reconstituted army. Friction between the army and the restored Bourbons, and between the people and the crown, meant that retaking power could well have widespread popular support. This situation was confirmed, at least in Napoleon's mind, when one of his former sub-prefects, Fleury de Chamboulon, brought him a message from Napoleon's former Foreign Minister, Hugh Maret. It claimed the people were "clamoring for Napoleon's return." Besides this positive news, Napoleon also learned of threats that the Royalists and allied governments were considering assassinating him or moving him to a more distant exile. The possibility of these threats being executed led to Napoleon's decision to return to France. After a little over nine months in exile, the Emperor was ready to seize power and return himself and the Empire to glory.

Taking advantage of a temporary absence of French and British Navy ships from Elba, Napoleon boarded the brig *Inconstant* and, with several hundred loyal men, returned to France. He landed at Golfe Juan on the Riviera on March 1, 1815, but his reception was less than overwhelming. In preparation for his return, Napoleon had issued proclamations to his former soldiers and the general public, which were also intended to influence the Congress of Vienna. One of these declarations read in part: "Soldiers! In my exile I heard your voice! I have arrived, despite all obstacles and perils! Your general, called to the throne by the people's choice and raised upon your shields, has been returned to you; come and join him . . . ."

To avoid Provence with its Royalist population, Bonaparte and his miniature army traveled the "Route Napoleon" through the Alps, picking up loyal soldiers along the way. These included the 5th Infantry Regiment and 7th Infantry Regiment, both of which joined him en masse, swelling his growing army's ranks. At Grenoble, Royalist troops sent to stop his advance confronted Napoleon's army. Unsure where their loyalties lay, Napoleon famously came to the front and exposed his breast to those soldiers, saying, "SOLDIERS! I am your Emperor. Do you not recognize me? If there is one among you who would kill his general, HERE I AM." This act of courage and bravado, so characteristic of Napoleon, moved these French soldiers to join his growing ranks instead of offering resistance.

A painting on ivory of Marshal Ney, dated 1810. This is part of a triptych that also included Napoleon and Marshal Murat.

Marshal Ney, previously one of Napoleon's main commanders, was serving the crown at this time. He recommended that Napoleon be brought to the capital in a cage, but apparently, Ney had second thoughts. On March 14, 1815, Ney joined Napoleon with 6,000 additional troops. Promising reforms and democratic elections, Napoleon marched into Paris on March 19, 1815, after the capital was vacated by a fleeing King Louis XVIII. Various noblemen and military commanders fell into line, and Napoleon's return to power was complete, at least in France.

Public acceptance of Napoleon's return—lukewarm at first—can be seen from this broadside, one of a series passed out on the streets in the weeks leading up to Napoleon's entry into Paris:

> The tiger has broken out of his den!
> The Ogre was three days at sea.
> The wretch has landed at Fréjus.
> The brigand has arrived at Antibes.
> The invader has reached Grenoble.
> The General has entered Lyons.
> Napoleon slept last night at Fontainebleau.
> The Emperor proceeds to the Tuileries today.
> His Imperial Majesty will address his loyal subjects tomorrow.

Napoleon started to reform the government. He set into motion plans to perpetuate a semi-democratic government along the lines of a constitutional monarchy that would take effect after his own death. That future government would include both hereditary nobles and popularly elected representatives, similar to the British Parliamentary model. In a plebiscite in which a disappointingly low number of voters participated, Napoleon's plan won a large majority, giving him a sense of confidence and legitimacy.

Meanwhile, both the Coalition allies and the French began preparations for the inevitable war to follow, as the allies were determined never to accept Napoleon's return to power. He was faced with a shrunken and depleted military force of only around 46,000 soldiers ready for combat, but by late May 1815, intense mobilization resulted in an increase of nearly 200,000 trained and equipped troops. Tens of thousands more were in depots, in the process of being trained and equipped. Anticipating an invasion by the Coalition forces, Napoleon organized an Armée du Nord as his main force, deploying other units around France for national defense.

Arrayed against France and Napoleon were Coalition forces from the Russian, Prussian, German, Austrian, Spanish, Dutch, Danish, Portuguese, Anglo-Sicilian and, of course, British armies. This massively superior force (with the exception of the Portuguese, who were not ready in time for combat), amounted to about a million men to face Napoleon's French and Neapolitan army of only around 280,000 men. The stage was set for a decisive battle that would settle the question of French government once and for all—or so it seemed at the time. Napoleon, branded an outlaw by the Coalition, deemed the main threat to come from Belgium and Germany, and so arrayed his heaviest forces to the north and east. Although France and Napoleon were, at least for the time, satisfied with the status quo, the Coalition was not. On March 13, 1815, the allies signed the Declaration of the Congress of Vienna, which stated their intent to rid Europe of Napoleon. This declaration was even signed by a French representative, Prince Talleyrand, Duke of Dalberg, a political chameleon who had been a Catholic bishop, turned to politics, and was defrocked by the pope. He served French administrations of every stripe, from Louis XVI to the Revolutionary government, then Napoleon, Louis XVIII, and Louis-Phillipe. Despite having been Napoleon's chief diplomat, Talleyrand smoothly segued into the role of facilitator of the Bourbon restoration. On March 25, the nations allied against Napoleon's France signed a treaty pledging to field an army of at least 150,000 men each, although Britain avoided that obligation by paying subsidies to nations better able to raise that manpower.

Engraving of Marshal Blücher produced shortly after his death in 1819.

The Coalition's two leading commanders, Marshal Blücher of Prussia and Britain's Duke of Wellington, were eager to commence the invasion of France. Nevertheless, the Coalition's leaders decided to delay the attack until July 1, when Austrian and Russian forces were prepared to join. Of course, this decision had the unwanted effect of allowing Napoleon and the French to prepare better defenses and/or make their own offensive plans. Although not wanting war, Napoleon was forced into it. He decided that a pre-emptive strike would surprise his enemies and catch allied armies before they were totally prepared for war. Napoleon hoped he could fight his scattered enemies as individual units before they could be massed against him. His strategy was to use local superiority of numbers to defeat the English and Prussians piecemeal.

On June 15, Napoleon's army crossed the Sambre River at Charleroi in what is now Belgium. His forces consolidated their position at Mont-Saint-Jean between the English-led forces to the west and Prussian-led allies to the east. This push across France's northern border thus preempted an invasion by the Coalition. Fighting commenced the next day, June 16, when Marshal Ney held off Wellington's English and allied army at Quatre Bras, and Napoleon led a force against Blücher, defeating the Prussians at the battle of Ligny. Ney had faced about 36,000 men under Wellington's command while fielding about 20,000 of his own, resulting in 4,800 casualties for the English and 4,140 for the French. Ney had accomplished his mission by preventing Wellington from reinforcing Blücher, but despite holding their own against superior odds, the French could not afford to match losses with the Coalition. Ligny was the larger battle, where Napoleon himself commanded 68,000 men of the Armée du Nord against 84,000 Coalition troops under Field Marshal Blücher.

The battle of Ligny was a disaster for the French, although on the surface Napoleon had won a tactical victory. His army suffered between 8,000 and 12,000 men killed and wounded, who could not be replaced. Blücher's losses were even greater–some 12,000 casualties and 8,000 deserters. Furthermore, they were forced to retreat after a failed counter-attack led by the 72-year-old Blücher himself, who was injured when his horse was shot and fell on him. Indeed, he could have been easily captured, but French forces did not realize who he was.

The French failed to capitalize on their success by allowing

Blücher's forces to escape mainly intact, and, ominously, retreat to the north instead of back to the east. Later, from their northern location, the Prussians would be better able to reinforce Wellington at Waterloo. Despite winning the field at Ligny, Napoleon had failed in his goal of rendering the Prussians impotent. On June 17, he headed west toward what he saw would be the decisive battle with Wellington, leaving the Marquis de Grouchy to pursue Blücher. Because of ambiguous orders, delays, and perhaps a lack of focus, Grouchy did not succeed in catching and destroying the retreating Prussians. That failure would prove crucial. Once again, French losses were a major factor in a war of attrition.

Both Wellington's and Blücher's forces had retreated north toward Brussels, with Wellington stopping to prepare defenses outside the Belgian town of Waterloo. On June 18, Napoleon's army attacked Wellington's English and allied forces there. This was the decisive battle of Napoleon's career as the leader of France.

The stage had been set for a climactic battle to take place on Sunday, June 18. A crushing victory by Napoleon's army might have resulted in a forced peace, perhaps permitting Bonaparte to reign throughout his normal life and establish the constitutional monarchy with his hereditary line. Success on the battlefield might also have convinced Austria to accept peace. Such a victory would have left Russia's army to face Napoleon *sans* allies, with a probable outcome of French victory, presuming the Russians did not seek peace instead. Of course, it is also possible that the allies would simply regroup and continue their fight against Napoleon. Conversely, a defeat at Waterloo seemed likely to mark the end or the beginning of the end of Napoleon's career as emperor of the French and the end of the French Empire he had built. The third possibility, a stalemate in which Napoleon's army was not destroyed, would have likely resulted in more combat until a future battle did prove decisive. Thus, the stakes were as high or higher than for any other battle Napoleon had ever faced. Victory was imperative. There were no alternatives. Wellington and Blücher must also have been well aware of the battle's monumental importance. All soldiers and officers on both sides were imbued with the dire need for maximum effort and sacrifice. That implied a hard-fought battle such as most of these men had not yet experienced.

The Duke of Wellington knew how formidable his opponent could be. He said Napoleon alone was "worth 40,000 men" on a battlefield. What he meant was Bonaparte's active participation in directing a battle under normal conditions. Napoleon would not, however, face his greatest battle in normal conditions, but in ill health, probably suffering from a stomach ulcer and severe hemorrhoids, which limited his ability to ride a horse to observe the battlefield and personally direct his troops. Napoleon's legendary energy and drive would not be a factor at Waterloo.

While Bonaparte and the French prepared to attack, Wellington readied his defenses, personally overseeing the planning. He arranged with Blücher to provide at least a corps in reinforcement so the English commander could be confident of mounting a well-prepared defense at Mont-Saint-Jean. Blücher had the men to spare, but the corps he had promised was exhausted from several days of marching and could not be on hand when the battle started. Blücher, however, did promise Wellington support from three other Prussian formations, allowing Wellington to battle where he stood instead of being forced to retreat farther north to Brussels. Those Prussian units moved slowly though, and the time of their arrival was uncertain.

While the English and allied forces prepared their defense, Napoleon hesitated. He delayed the start of his attack due to the battlefield's muddy conditions, likely to negate the use of his superior cavalry and artillery. He might not have been so tentative, however, had he been aware of the Prussians' movement toward the battle. Napoleon expected to defeat Wellington separately and only afterward to deal with the Prussians.

French forces numbered about 73,000 men, of which over 14,000 were cavalry, and another 8,000 were artillery and engineers. Bonaparte boasted about 252 guns. He faced 68,000 Anglo-allied troops with only 156 guns. Believing these British troops were substandard and under-equipped, an assessment Wellington shared, Napoleon thought victory was highly achievable if not probable. Of course, this confidence did not take into account having to face 50,000 Prussian and allied reinforcements. Bonaparte erroneously believed the Prussians to have been defeated and disorganized.

The attack finally started sometime between 10 a.m. and 11:30 a.m. The fog of war makes it impossible to determine the precise starting time. The English and their allies repeatedly repulsed the French, but the relentless attacks were wearing Wellington's army down. His partial use of a reverse slope defense protected some of his troops from Napoleon's superior artillery, while the soft, rain-soaked ground absorbed many of the cannonballs, limiting their effectiveness.

While the British were being ground down, Napoleon noticed an ominous sight: the Prussian advance guard approaching from his right. He sent orders to Grouchy to intercept these enemy reinforcements while they were still three hours marching time away, about five miles. But following his previous orders, Grouchy had been pursuing the Prussians from behind. He could not re-deploy in a blocking position. Napoleon's written order would not reach Grouchy until about 8 o'clock that evening, too late for action. Well before then, however, a subordinate beseeched Grouchy to march as quickly as possible to "the sound of guns" and provide Napoleon immediate assistance. Grouchy, meanwhile, kept to his previous orders and continued harassing the rear of the Prussian column.

As the French attack began to make inroads into the Coalition lines, Wellington committed two brigades of cavalry into the breach. This wild, ill-considered charge resulted in mass casualties among the English horsemen. At around 4 p.m., Marshal Ney mistook an evacuation of wounded in the center of the British defense line for a retreat. He sent his remaining cavalry, about 9,000 men, in a bid to exploit that "retreat." Napoleon saw this and lamented that the charge had come "an hour too soon." A lack of coordination between

French artillery and cavalry diminished the attack's effectiveness. Although determined, the French cavalry were mauled by English artillery firing at close range. Ney saw the failure of his cavalry attack, and called on his remaining infantry reserves to mount another assault. The tide seemed to turn in favor of the French. Many of Wellington's lieutenants were killed in the close combat, and French victory appeared to be imminent. A Dutch cavalry unit ordered to attack fled the battlefield. To all appearances, a great victory for Napoleon was in hand.

At this crucial juncture, the Prussians appeared in the late afternoon, forcing Napoleon to divert some of his forces to protect his flank from Blücher instead of making a final blow against Wellington. With the moment of critical opportunity quickly slipping away, Napoleon had to commit his final reserve, the Imperial Guard, at about 7:30 p.m. This was his last-ditch bid for victory. The attack failed, and Napoleon's defeat was now inevitable. He had lost the battle and perhaps 26,000 men killed or wounded, with another 7,000 captured and 15,000 deserters. His army and his future as an emperor were no more.

The next day, June 19, Grouchy doggedly followed Napoleon's orders and kept attacking the Prussians, finally defeating them at Wavre. This was a hollow victory, after Grouchy's failure to arrive with his 33,000 troops had cost France the war. While Napoleon toyed with the idea of resisting, perhaps again leading the army against the oncoming allies, in the end, he faced reality. His last act as emperor was to issue his abdication:

> Declaration to the French People
>
> Frenchmen, in commencing the war to maintain national independence, I counted on the union of all efforts, of all wills and on the assistance of all the national authorities. I felt justified in hoping for success, and defied all the declarations of the powers against me.
>
> The circumstances appear to have changed.
>
> I offer myself as a sacrifice to the hatred of the enemies

of France. May they be sincere in their declarations and only desire my person!

My political life is finished, and I proclaim my son, under the title of Napoleon II, Emperor of the French.

The present ministers will form provisionally the council of government. The interest I carry for my son causes me to ask the Chambers to organize, without delay, a regency by law.

All of you unite for the public good, for remaining an independent nation.

At the Élysée Palace, 22 June 1815.

Napoleon

Engraving dated 1817 of Napoleon surrendering to Captain Maitland aboard the Bellerophon.

Napoleon wanted to escape to the United States. Indeed, while still in Paris he had directed General Bertrand to apply for passports to travel to America and arranged to have two ships available at Rochefort for the Atlantic crossing. But he delayed the journey, first at his old home of Malmaison, then in his trip south, and finally in Rochefort and the Isle d'Aix. He eventually realized that he was blockaded by the Royal Navy and had to consider other options. Bonaparte's brother Joseph had joined him in Rochefort, making arrangements to sail from a different port; he offered to switch places with Napoleon to allow the emperor an easy escape, given their similar appearances. But Napoleon declined this offer and all other options. He surrendered to Captain Maitland of the HMS *Bellerophon* on July 15. Napoleon's return to power, which became known as the Hundred Days, was over. French resistance continued until September, but the Treaty of Paris officially ended hostilities in November 1815, once again restoring the Bourbon throne. Napoleon was stripped of his imperial title and exiled to the remote island of St. Helena in the South Atlantic Ocean, from which he would never return alive.

9. A Murder on St. Helena? — The Final Exile and Death of Napoleon (1815-1821)

Determined not to allow a repeat of the Hundred Days, or of the failure of Napoleon's first exile on Elba, the British and their allies decided to send the deposed emperor to the remote South Atlantic island of St. Helena. There, the nearest land is the coast of Africa, 1,162 miles away, and any attempted escape would be much more difficult than from Elba. Instead of an easy 30 miles from Corsica, and just over 600 miles from Paris, reaching St. Helena required a long sea voyage. Napoleon would find few visitors willing to travel to such a remote location, thus also keeping him away from prying eyes.

With only a tiny cadre of loyal followers to accompany him, Napoleon did not have the small army and navy that had been at his disposal on Elba. The only military force on St. Helena–which only had about 3,500 inhabitants–was British. Stripped of his title and his small military force, Bonaparte was isolated and at the mercy of his British captors. Their account of his exile would be the only official story, not open to independent review, a situation guaranteed to create conspiracy theories when, just six years later, Napoleon would die at just 51, of no universally accepted cause. Yet, some of his companions did write extensively about their experiences on St. Helena and of their lengthy interviews with Napoleon. Conditions on the bleak island were dank and damp. With little to stimulate the mind of such a driven man, Napoleon languished in his exile, complaining of the conditions, food, and accommodations. It is generally believed that these factors caused his early demise. Others have postulated more sinister forces behind his death, or murder, as some historians believe.

Napoleon's second exile was to be decidedly more miserable than his first. Far from France and in a disagreeable climate, St. Helena was off most of the major sea-lanes. That made it an unlikely destination or stopover for shipping. The fallen emperor's retinue found the accommodations, with their low ceilings and shabby rooms, less than appropriate for the man who once ruled France and conquered much of Europe. While Napoleon's first exile carefully maintained the decorum acceded to a monarch, it was clear that this second expulsion was punitive. There was no doubt that Napoleon was a prisoner. But even during the 10-week voyage to the desolate island, he managed to keep his spirits up.

Half the size of Elba, St. Helena was not prepared for the deposed emperor's arrival. His quarters in the mountain village of Longwood were not yet finished, leaving him to room with a British family until his new home was complete. The island's British governor, Sir Hudson Lowe, held Napoleon in a contempt that he did not try to conceal. Lowe would not call Napoleon "Your Majesty," referring to him instead as "General Bonaparte." Napoleon was insulted by British insistence that he not be allowed to ride without a British escort and that he show himself to a British orderly every day.

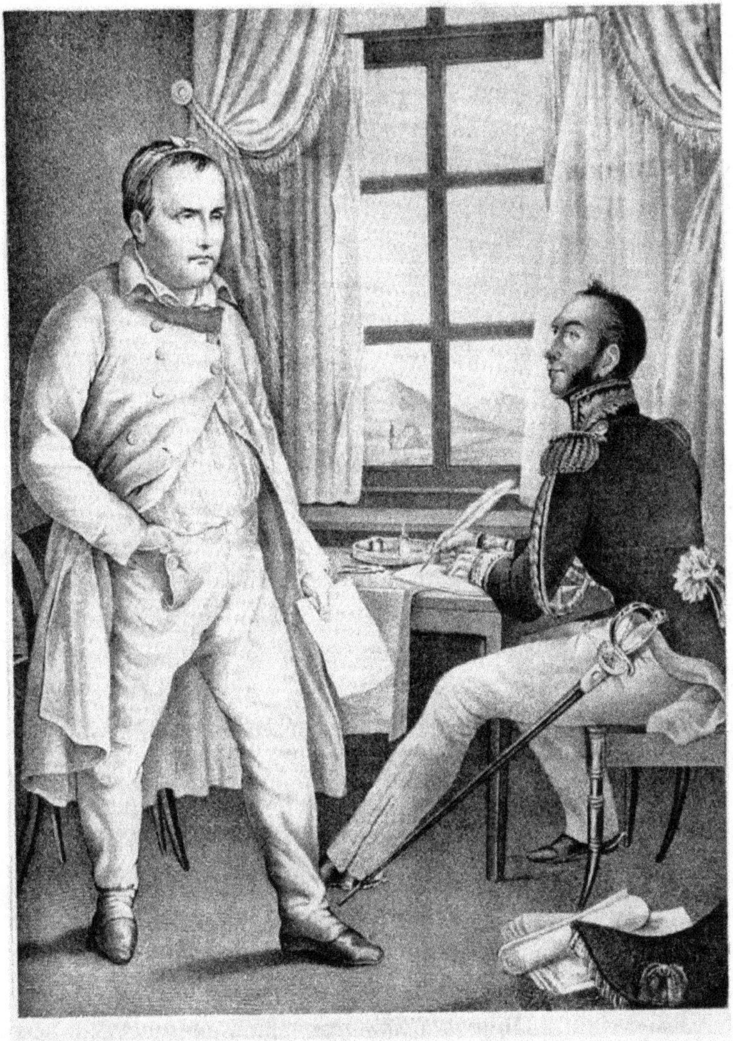

NAPOLEON DICTATING TO GOURGAUD

From a lithograph after Steuben

19th-century engraving showing Napoleon dictating his memoirs to General Gourgaud.

Spending much of his time writing memoirs and brooding, Napoleon complained of shabby treatment. Perhaps he should have been thankful that the monarchies of the time generally forbade the execution of defeated enemy rulers. Kings and emperors were deathly afraid of setting a precedent that revolutionaries might use against them. To put his complaints in perspective, Napoleon's retinue was provided with a substantial daily allotment of 17 bottles of wine to wash down their nine chickens and 40 kilograms of meat. This portion was in addition to whatever Champagne and distilled spirits were deemed appropriate for each day.

Perhaps Napoleon's best friend on St. Helena was the young daughter of the Balcombe family with whom he had lived while the house at Longwood was being prepared. Lucia Elizabeth Balcombe, best known as Betsy, was born in 1802 in St. Helena, but educated in England, where she learned fluent French. Returning to St. Helena in 1814, she was there with her family to welcome the exiled emperor into their household the following year. Her friendship with Napoleon was obvious which, along with her family's cordial relationship with the former emperor, caused Governor Lowe some level of suspicion.

Even Napoleon's staff was somewhat envious of Betsy, who continued to visit Napoleon after the move to Longwood. She would call him "Boney" to his face, and Napoleon seemed not to mind at all, let alone reprimand the girl. The press in both England and France speculated about a romantic attachment between this unlikely pair, but Betsy and the Balcombes left St. Helena in 1818. The young lady married in 1821, but Betsy maintained contact with the Bonaparte family for the rest of her life. Napoleon's best friend in exile died at the age of 69 in 1871.

Of course, conspirators had not waited for Napoleon's exile on St. Helena to plot his murder. It is likely that French Royalists, Jacobins, usurpers, and foreign—that is to say English—assassins had all planned at various times and for various reasons to do away with the emperor. These plots and attempts lend a great degree of credibility to the belief held by some to this day that Napoleon was indeed murdered while on St. Helena.

One notable plot that nearly came to fruition took place on Christmas Eve, 1800, when Royalist plotters staged a wagon containing a barrel of gunpowder along the likely path of a carriage taking Napoleon to the opera. Possibly because of the speed of Bonaparte's carriage, the gunpowder was set off a moment too late, and Napoleon survived the blast unharmed, although as many as 52 unintended victims did not. One of those unfortunates was a girl the plotters hired to hold the reins of the horse hitched to the powder-laden wagon, a measure of the conspirators' cold-blooded nature. Wounded in that attack was Hortense Beauharnais, Josephine's daughter, who was riding in a carriage following Napoleon's. Hortense's injuries brought home to the Bonapartes the dangers of life in power. Napoleon had often teased Josephine with stories of conspiracies, attempts on his life, or kidnapping plots. Considering this incident, it is easy to see how she could believe him! Despite blaming Jacobin extremists, deflecting blame from the Royalists, Napoleon did have two of the main ringleaders executed. This near-miss occurred only months after a previous attempt was foiled by a conspirator who was secretly providing Bonaparte with information. The plan was to stab Napoleon, giving the plot the name The Dagger Conspiracy.

Another documented incident was an attempt to poison Napoleon by replacing his snuff with poison, which of course failed, leading those conspirators to plot Napoleon's kidnapping. In 1804, another kidnapping scheme, known as the Cadoudal Plot, also failed, which resulted in numerous imprisonments and executions, including two of Napoleon's generals. Recent evidence indicates that the British government and French Royalists were involved in the conspiracy, and that the word "abduction" was just a euphemism for murder.

Napoleon's police minister, Joseph Fouché, had kept Napoleon aware of plots against him, and at one time reported that 10 of them were known. No wonder it is so easy to speculate that Napoleon's death may have been murder. Another piece of evidence that assassination theorists cite is that 25 years after his death, Napoleon's body was remarkably well preserved. His casket was opened on St. Helena, and the body's condition suggested that a large amount of arsenic—a common poison for the time—may have been in his system. A 20th-century Swedish physician and self-styled toxicologist, Sten Forshufvud, published a book in 1961 alleging that Napoleon had been poisoned by a long-term application of arsenic, a deliberate murder. In 1983, an English adaptation of Forshufvud's allegations was published, called *Assassination on St. Helena: The Murder of Napoleon Bonaparte.* It followed a book by the renowned Napoleonic scholar Ben Weider (of the body-building family) and David Hapgood called *The Murder of Napoleon.* That 1982 work used the ideas Forshufvud had put forward.

These three authors and other Napoleon aficionados arranged to have several strands of Napoleon's hair tested for the presence of arsenic. A lab found the levels of the deadly poison to be around 38 times higher than average. Sending the samples to another laboratory in Scotland yielded the same result, supporting the theory of arsenic poisoning. The different hairs that were tested came from different periods in the last five years of Napoleon's life, and contained varying amounts of the poison, indicating uneven ingestion of the arsenic. That lessens the possibility that the arsenic found in Napoleon's system was introduced environmentally. The theory of a systematic course of poisoning led to a suspicion that one of Napoleon's French attendants, Charles Tristan, marquis de Montholon, was the guilty party. This man was a military officer of dubious credentials. He makes a convenient suspect, one with ready access to Napoleon and the ability to carry out the plot. Other modern historians have come to accept at least the strong possibility that Napoleon was murdered this way.

Interestingly, many French patriots and scholars strongly disagree with the idea that a Frenchman could have murdered Napoleon, and do not accept this theory as fact. They assume that if the Emperor had indeed been poisoned, the conspirators would have been English.

The true cause of Napoleon's death remains in question. The medical and other evidence is not 100 percent conclusive. The great man may have simply died of natural causes that may or may not have been aggravated by ignorant medical care. Or Napoleon may have died of poisoning. If the Emperor had been poisoned by arsenic, this poison might have been introduced purposefully. It could also have been by unintentional but just as deadly as accidental means. It seems likely the debate will not be settled any time soon, and readers are left to decide for themselves which explanation of Napoleon's death seems most plausible.

A pressed wood period snuffbox showing Napoleon's burial on St Helena. The inside of the lid shows Napoleon in happier days.

Whatever the cause, Napoleon died shortly before 6 p.m. on May 5, 1821. He was given military honors, and on May 9, with bands playing and artillery salutes, he was buried in St. Helena's Geranium Valley, where he had often spent time alone. Disputes about what should be written on his tombstone were not resolved, and it was left blank.

Pressed horn snuffbox circa 1840, showing Napoleon's casket on St Helena being opened prior to its removal to Paris.

The saga of his death was not yet over, however. In July 1840, King Louis Philippe sent his son to exhume Napoleon's body and return it to France. Once on the French shores, the body was taken by boat up the Seine River to Paris. Thousands of people paid their respects along the way. In 1861, Napoleon's body was moved to its permanent resting place, in a huge casket under the dome of Les Invalides, a complex of military museums and monuments. This fulfilled his wish to be buried "on the banks of the Seine, amongst the French people whom I have loved so well."

Napoleon's legacy, however, extends far beyond being the subject of a captivating murder mystery. Nearly 200 years after his death on St. Helena, Napoleon is remembered much more for the accomplishments of his life than the circumstances of his death.

10. Napoleon's Legacy

Seldom in history does a man come along who leaves such a lasting impression on the world as did Napoleon Bonaparte. Not only did he impact the Western world more than any man of his time, but he also left a legacy equaled by few others, as evidenced by the distinction of possibly having more written about him than any other person in history aside from perhaps Jesus. Scholars are in disagreement here, as some sources give the distinction to Jesus, others to Napoleon; doing our own title search on WorldCat suggests that the distinction should probably go to Jesus, although there are at least tens of thousands of books about Napoleon. That is about twice as many as about such other oft-written-about historical figures as even Adolf Hitler.

Depicted in much of British and other non-French literature as a small and egoistical man, the caricature of a spoiled-brat despot, the true Napoleon was nothing of the sort. Despite the unflattering legacy depicted by those who revile him, Napoleon was not the cartoonish character often shown as a pouting, tantrum-throwing imp. Nor was Bonaparte the Anti-Christ or the herald of the apocalypse. History is written by the winners, and thus Napoleon's legacy has been besmirched by his enemies and those enemies' heirs. Often depicted as an abnormally short man, Napoleon, who stood at about five feet six inches, was not tall, but was around average height for his day. Still, his legacy includes the term "Napoleonic Complex" (also called "Napoleon Complex," "Short Man Complex or Syndrome" or even "Little Man Syndrome"). This condition is attributed to Napoleon as overcompensating for his allegedly tiny stature by an exaggerated aggressiveness and show of bravado. This caricature was initially promoted by British cartoonists. For many today, however falsely, this image may well be the context in which Napoleon is most remembered.

A period engraving showing Napoleon's past glory.

More substantial elements of Napoleon's legacy can be found in our everyday world, such as the nearly universal system of measurements known as the metric system. Adopted by France in 1799 under Napoleon's leadership, the metric system was spread to all the lands conquered by France during the Napoleonic Era and later to France's overseas empire. The system's simplicity and logic quickly caught on, eventually making it a worldwide system of weights and measures. Oddly enough, the United States is the only major industrialized nation not to embrace the metric system, although it was approved for use in the U.S. in 1866. Today, the U.S. uses a mix of metric and non-metric standards, with the military and the auto industry being almost exclusively metric.

Napoleon was acutely aware of history and science. His forays into such research during the Egyptian expedition of 1799 resulted in the discovery of the Rosetta Stone, an inscribed tablet dating to 196 BC with text in ancient Egyptian hieroglyphics, Demotic, and ancient Greek. Prior to this find, researchers had no way of deciphering Egyptian hieroglyphs. The stone's three scripts, with essentially the same text in three writing systems, allowed for accurate translation of hieroglyphs for the first time. The Rosetta Stone served as a decoding key that has allowed deep insight into ancient Egyptian culture. Today the term "Rosetta Stone" is synonymous with "decoding key" or as a metaphor for the clue that unlocks a great mystery.

The spread of French culture through Napoleon's conquests introduced the ideas and reforms of the French Revolution to other countries. None of these was as important or lasting as the Napoleonic Code, a system of civil laws and legal philosophy that replaced the convoluted tangle of confusing, inconsistent legal systems found in pre-Napoleonic Europe. These often contradictory and unfair legal systems were founded in feudal tradition and locally convenient laws that had been tailored to the benefit of those in charge. The result was a patchwork of unjust and baffling rules that promised little prospect for any real justice other than for the rich and powerful. The Napoleonic Code provided much of Europe with a model of modernized law and legal procedure. It emphasized clear and consistent procedures and remedies that applied to all persons equally, a novel idea at the time. "The Rule of Law" replaced "The Rule of Man" and has been the standard of modern legal systems ever since. The Napoleonic Code embraced such concepts familiar to Americans but unknown to much of Europe at the time as "presumed innocent until proven guilty" and a defendant's right to legal counsel. England, for example, did not provide a right to legal counsel until 1836. The vast influence of the Napoleonic Code covered not only much of Europe, where it persists today, but also the European nation's colonies, many of which as independent countries still have legal systems founded on the principles of the Napoleonic Code. In the United States, because of the state's history as a former French colony, the Napoleonic Code is found in Louisiana. Unfortunately, one part of the legacy of the Napoleonic Code was the relegation of wives to a subordinate legal status *vis-à- vis* their husbands. That concept, common at the time, has been perpetuated at least in part by the Napoleonic code's broad adoption.

Napoleon's legacy also lives on in military circles. His leadership is studied and emulated in such places as the military academies at West Point and Sandhurst. The Duke of Wellington, the general who defeated Napoleon at Waterloo, said Napoleon's presence on the battlefield was worth 40,000 men in the field. (That statement has been paraphrased from several slightly differing quotations). The emperor's willingness to share danger with his men is a trait shared with successful military commanders to this day, while those who lead from the rear are more likely to fail. Napoleon had been wounded in battle twice, by bayonet and by artillery shell, and had a whopping 19 horses shot out from under him! These examples, combined with his men's legendary devotion, are points drilled into officer trainees even today.

Napoleon is sometimes quoted as saying that "an army marches on its stomach," showing his great attention to his men's needs and recognizing the importance of logistics in combat. To that end, the great commander ordered that a method of preparing and keeping palatable rations be developed to feed his soldiers in the field. That spawned the use of "canning" to preserve field rations, originally soup sealed in wine bottles, providing his men with superior field rations: the direct ancestor of today's MREs.

Napoleon had trees planted along French roads so his soldiers would have shade while marching. He instituted the Legion of Honor to recognize those men who showed extreme bravery and élan, a method of recognition we see today in awarding of military medals. The Legion of Honor was also bestowed, as it still is today, on civilians who especially deserve recognition. Another of Napoleon's lasting contributions to military culture is that of battlefield evacuation and prompt treatment of wounded soldiers, an innovative concept at the time, now taken for granted. The grand Arc de Triomphe in Paris stands as mute testimony to the importance Napoleon placed in the pantheon of French heroes. After the Eiffel Tower, his arch is possibly the most iconic landmark in Paris.

Bonaparte's great legacy also covers his greatest foes, with the Duke of Wellington and Lord Admiral Nelson having earned their place among Britain's greatest war heroes at Napoleon's expense. If it is true that a great hero must have a great enemy, these English heroes could have had no greater foil than the Corsican emperor. In fact, the English saw fit to rename the most vibrant part of their capital, London, Trafalgar Square in honor of Nelson's great victory over Napoleon's fleet. Also in London, Waterloo Bridge and Waterloo station stand as tributes to Wellington's triumph 10 years after Trafalgar.

The term "Waterloo" has become an unfortunate legacy of Napoleon, used as a synonym for "catastrophic or decisive defeat." Without that famous battle, most of us would probably not be aware of the little Belgian town, now a Brussels suburb of nearly 30,000 people. Numerous towns and cities in the United States are also named "Waterloo," although the U.S. did not have a hand in the battle. For that matter, one will find numerous other places in the United States named after Napoleon or Bonaparte. Even the Mexican commander General Antonio Lopez de Santa Ana, the anti-hero of the 1836 siege of the Alamo and of the Mexican-

American War a decade later, was known as "The Napoleon of the West." Sports stars such as Napoleon Lajoie, a baseball Hall-of-Famer, and Napoleon McCallum, in the College Football Hall of Fame, have borne the emperor's name. A character from *The Man from* U.N.C.L.E television series and movie, Napoleon Solo, has likewise shared that distinction.

Of course, Louis-Napoleon Bonaparte, known better as Napoleon III, emperor of the Second French Empire from 1852 to 1870 (after serving as the Second Republic's president from 1848 to 1852) was Napoleon's nephew. Napoleon's own son and would-be royal heir, Napoleon II, had died at age 21 after twice being emperor in name only for just a few days as a child. It is for Napoleon III that the "Napoleon Gun" or "Napoleon Cannon" is named. That highly effective 12-pound howitzer could fire an exploding projectile, solid shot, canister, and other available ammunition. It was the primary cannon used by both sides during the American Civil War and was also Britain's main land-based artillery of the period. The gun was one of the last to be cast in bronze. The French called their version "Canon Obusier de 12," while the English called theirs "12-Pounder Napoleon Model of 1857."

The royal lineage of Napoleon I died out. His blood no longer flows in the veins of modern European royalty. Josephine, his first wife and ex-empress of the French, does have a considerable genetic legacy among today's European aristocracy, with numerous crowned heads and others of the noble class descended from Napoleon's one true love.

Not surprisingly, a man with so much influence on world events and such a dashing historical figure, both admired and reviled, would leave an enormous legacy in cultural matters. Literature teems with factual and fictional accounts of Napoleon and his adventures, often from the perspective of those who fought against him. Tolstoy's epic 1869 novel *War and Peace*, seeing Napoleon from a Russian point of view, certainly ranks near the top of this list, as do many of the English sea-faring tales such as the *Horatio Hornblower* series of novels that C. S. Forester wrote from 1937 to 1967. Both fictionalized and historical movies have been made from Napoleon's life and battles, both for the motion picture screen and television. Epic productions have dramatized *War and Peace* for movies, television, and opera.

Films depicting Napoleon rank among some of the finest achievements in cinematic history. Abel Gance's 1927 *Napoléon* is considered one of the silent era's greatest masterpieces. *Désirée*, released in 1954, based on the best-selling 1951 novel of the same name, stars legendary actor Marlon Brando as Napoleon. It was nominated for two Academy Awards. *Waterloo* (1970), starring the acclaimed actors Rod Steiger as Napoleon and Christopher Plummer as Wellington, won two BAFTA Awards and one David di Donatello Award, in addition to being novelized. The 2002 Emmy Award-winning *Napoleon* miniseries was at the time the most expensive television miniseries produced in Europe, costing the equivalent of $46,330,000. It was so successful, widely airing internationally, that in 2002 Atari released a video game based on the miniseries. Napoleon has appeared as a character in over 400 films, with more still scheduled for release or in production.

As mentioned earlier, in addition to numerous films about Napoleon's life, to list all the books written about him would require an entire book of its own! Napoleon's portrayal in popular culture goes beyond books and films. References and allusions to him are found in all sorts of other cultural expressions not explicitly about the emperor, in books, plays, songs, animated cartoons (perhaps the most memorable being Napoleon Bonafrog on *Teenage Mutant Ninja Turtles*), video games (including *Assassins' Creed*), and numerous cameo appearances. One of these was in the 1989 film *Bill and Ted's Excellent Adventure*, in which two high school boys go through time collecting historical figures for a school project, including Bonaparte himself. That movie, in turn, spun off animated and live-action television, comic book, and video game adaptations.

Tchaikovsky's wonderful 1812 *Overture*, from 1880, is perhaps the greatest music associated with Napoleon, commemorating the

Russian victory over the *Grande Armée*. Ludwig von Beethoven was allegedly planning to dedicate his *Third Symphony* to Napoleon in his revolutionary role as first consul, but he angrily rescinded this honor when Napoleon declared himself emperor of the French. In Beethoven's eyes, Napoleon had betrayed the ideals of the French Revolution. If classical music is not your cup of tea, you may be more familiar with the ABBA tune "Waterloo" from 1974 or the 1949 American country song "Bonaparte's Retreat" by Pee Wee King. More recently and perhaps even most bizarrely, an epic rap battle featuring Napoleon has received over 48 million views on YouTube, showing Napoleon's appeal even to today's youth! Indeed, Napoleon's musical legacy has affected practically all genres of music for the past two centuries.

Also on the lighter side, Bonaparte graces us with the legacy of Napoleon Brandy and the high-quality Napoleon Cognac, as well as the Bigarreau Napoleon cherry, perhaps the ancestor of the Bing cherry, used to make Maraschino cherries. Napoleon olive oil is of the highest quality. The delicious French pastry known as the Napoleon (alternately called by its French name, Mille-feuille) may not even be named after Napoleon himself, but perhaps after the Italian city of Naples. We prefer to think of it as the sweetest legacy of the great man who himself was not always so sweet.

Even with foodstuffs, Napoleon's enemies owe their epicurean legacy to their fame earned while fighting the emperor, with the Lord Nelson Apple named after the hero of Trafalgar and Beef Wellington (perhaps) for the victor at Waterloo. (The dish's connection with Arthur Wellesley, Duke of Wellington, is not a sure thing, notwithstanding Woody Allen's jokes about this in *Love and Death*, his 1975 parody of *War and Peace*). We are sure that the Marshal Ney pastry is indeed named after the French Marshal Michel Ney, who Napoleon called "The Bravest of the Brave."

Finally, Napoleon retains a strong "fan" following among both scholars and laypersons. Among the most notable groups dedicated to Napoleonic history are The International Napoleonic Society and The Napoleonic Historical Society. The Canadian author, businessman and World War II veteran Ben Weider, who lived from 1923 to 2008, founded the International Society. The noted historian J. David Markham, this book's co-author, is its current president. Both men have received many international awards and honors, have written numerous books, and have frequently appeared in television documentaries about Napoleonic history. The Napoleonic Historical Society, in which Markham also plays a prominent leadership role, technically was created in 2006, but its origins go back much earlier. It is the descendant of the Napoleonic Society of America, created in 1983 by businessman and World War II veteran Robert Snibbe, who died in 2004. Similar organizations dedicated to Napoleon and his era have existed and continue to exist around the world. These groups have numerous members of diverse ages and genders from many countries around the world. They hold conferences in various places associated with Napoleonic history from North America to Europe to the Middle East!

Snuffbox circa 1825 showing Alexander the Great and Julius Caesar welcoming Napoleon and the 'heroes of the 19th century' to the Elysian Fields.

Indeed, Napoleon Bonaparte touched the lives of millions of people in his day and many millions since. He was one of history's most influential people. Although blamed for wars and destruction, often not his real goal but the product of his less far-seeing enemies,

Napoleon's positive legacy certainly outweighs any of the bad that can be attributed to him. His shadow today covers at least half the world. Who would have thought that the boy whose mother once spanked him for ridiculing his grandmother would become one of history's most memorable men?

Sources

Abbott, John Stevens Cabot. *Napoleon at St. Helena: Or, Interesting Anecdotes and Remarkable Conversations of the Emperor During the Five and a Half Years of His Captivity*. New York: Harper & Brothers, 1871.

Adkins, Roy. *Trafalgar: The Biography of a Battle*. Boston: Little Brown, 2004.

Aaslestad, Katherine B. and Johan Joor, eds. *Revisiting Napoleon's Continental System: Local, Regional and European Experiences*. London: Palgrave Macmillan UK, 2015.

Alison, Sir Archibald. *History of Europe: From the Commencement of the French Revolution in* M.DCC.LXXXIX *to the Restoration of the Bourbons in* M.DCCC.XV, Vol. III. Paris: Baudry's European library, 1841.

Balcombe Abell, Lucia Elizabeth. To *Befriend an Emperor: Betsy Balcombe's Memoirs of Napoleon on* St. *Helena, with an introduction by J. David Markham*. Welwyn Garden City, UK: Ravenhall, 2005.

Barbero, Alessandro. *The Battle: A New History of the Battle of Waterloo*, tr. John Cullen. London: Atlantic Books, 2006.

Bell, David A. *Napoleon: A Concise Biography*. Oxford and New York: Oxford University Press, 2015.

Bingham, D.A. A *Selection from the Letters and Despatches of the First Napoleon, with Explanatory* Notes. London: Chapman and Hall, Limited, 1884.

Bonaparte, Napoleon. *Copies of Original Letters From the Army of General Bonaparte in Egypt, Intercepted by the Fleet Under the Command of Admiral Lord Nelson*. London: Printed for J. Wright, Opposite Old Bond Street, Piccadilly, 1798.

Bonaparte, Napoleon. *Correspondance Générale publiée par la Fondation Napoléon*. Paris: Éditions Fayard, 2004-2016.

Bonaparte, Napoleon. *Letters of Napoleon to Josephine*. Ed. Léon Cerf, trans. Henry Bunn. New York: Brentano's, 1931.

Bonaparte, Napoleon. *Napoleon's Letters*, edited and translated by J. M. Thompson. London: PRION, 1998.

Burnham, Robert. "The British Expeditionary Force to Walcheren: 1809," *The Napoleon Series*, http://www.napoleon-series.org/military/battles/c_walcheren.html (accessed December 29, 2016).

Carlyle, Thomas. *The French Revolution: A History*. New York: American Book Exchange, 1881.

Caulaincourt, General Armand Augustin Louis, marquis de, duc de Vicence, *With Napoleon in Russia*. From the orig. edn. By Jean Hanoteau. Abridged, Edited, and with an Introduction by George Libaire. (New York: William Morrow and Company, 1935).

Censer Jack R. and Lynn Hunt. *Liberty, Equality, and Fraternity: Exploring the French Revolution*. University Park: The Pennsylvania State University Press, 2004.

Chandler, David. *The Campaigns of Napoleon*. New York: Scribner, 1966.

Chandler, David G. *The Campaigns of Napoleon*. New York: Simon and Schuster, 2009.

Chandler, David G. *The Campaigns of Napoleon*, Volume I. Simon and Schuster, 2009.

Cornwell, Bernard. *Waterloo: The History of Four Days, Three Armies and Three Battles*. New York: HarperCollins, 2015.

Cronin, Vincent. *Napoleon Bonaparte: An Intimate Biography*. New York: William Morrow & Company, 1972.

Dietrich, William. *Napoleon's Rules: Life and Career Lessons from Bonaparte*. Burrows Publishing, 2015.

"Documents Upon Napoleon and Education," *The Napoleon Series*, http://www.napoleon-series.org/research/government/legislation/c_education.html#sectionb (accessed August 27, 2016).

Dwyer, Philip. *Citizen Emperor: Napoleon in Power*. New Haven and London: Yale University Press, 2013.

Dwyer, Philip. *Napoleon and Europe*. London and New York: Routledge, 2014.

Dwyer, Philip. *Napoleon: The Path to Power 1769–1799*. London: A & C Black, 2014.

Erickson, Carolly. *Josephine: A Life of the Empress*. Macmillan, 2000.

Esdaile, Charles. *The Peninsular War: A New History*. New York: St. Martin's Press, 2015.

Esdaile, Charles. *Women in the Peninsular War*. Norman: University of Oklahoma Press, 2014.

Foa, Eugénie. *The Boy Life Of Napoleon*. Boston: Lothrop Publishing Company, 1895.

Fleming, Thomas. "Napoléon's Invasion of North America: *Aedes aegypti* takes a holiday, 1802," *What If? 2*, ed. Robert Cowley (New York: Berkley Books, 2002), 134-151.

Forrest, Alan. *Napoleon: Life, Legacy, and Image: A Biography*. New York: St. Martin's Press, 2012.

Forshufvud, Sten. *Who Killed Napoleon?* Tr. Alan Houghton Brodrick. London: Hutchinson, 1962.

Fournier, August. *Napoleon I: A Biography, Volume I*, Second Edition translated by Annie Elizabeth Adams. New York: Longmans, Green and Company, 1912.

Fournier, August. *Napoleon the First: A Biography*. Ed. Edward Gaylord Bourne, Tr. Margaret Bacon Corwin and Arthur Dart Bissell. New York: Henry Holt, 1903.

Fox, Charles James. *Napoleon Bonaparte and the Siege of Toulon*. Washington, D.C.: Law Reporter Company, 1902.

François, Charles. *Journal du capitaine François: dit le Dromadaire d'Egypte* 1792-1830. Paris: Tallandier, 2003.

George, Christopher T. "The Eroica Riddle: Did Napoleon Remain Beethoven's 'Hero?'"*Napoleonic Scholarship: The Journal of the International Napoleonic Society* 1.2 (December 1998), http://www.napoleon-series.org/ins/scholarship98/c_eroica.html (accessed 2 June 2016).

Gregorovius, Ferdinand. *Corsica in Its Picturesque, Social, and Historical Aspects: The Record of a Tour in the Summer of 1852*. London: Longman, Brown, Green, and Longmans, 1855.

Gruyer, Paul. *Napoleon, King of Elba*. Philadelphia: J.B. Lippincott, 1906.

Gueniffey, Patrice. *Bonaparte*: 1769-1802. Trans. Steven Rendell. Cambridge: Harvard University Press, 2015.

Hapgood, David and Ben Weider. *The Murder of Napoleon*. New York: Congdon and Lattes, Inc., 1982.

Henty, George A. At *Aboukir and Acre*: A *Story of Napoleon's Invasion of Egypt*. Tucson: Fireship Press, 2010.

Hochschild, Adam. *Bury the Chains: Prophets and Rebels in the Fight to Free an Empire's Slaves*. Boston and New York: Houghton Mifflin Harcourt, 2005.

James, William and Robert O'Byrne. *James' Naval History:* A *Narrative of the Naval Battles, Single Ship Actions, Notable Sieges And Dashing Cutting-out Expeditions Fought in the Days of Howe, Hood, Duncan, St. Vincent, Bridport, Nelson, Camperdown, Exmouth, Duckworth and Sir Sydney Smith*. London: W. H. Allen & Company, 1888.

Jones, Edwyn Henry Stuart. *The Last Invasion of Britain*. University of Wales Press, 1950.

Karsh, Inari. *Empires of the Sand: The Struggle for Mastery in the Middle East*, 1789–1923. Harvard University Press, 2001.

Landau, Elaine. *Napoleon Bonaparte*. Minneapolis: Twenty-First Century Books, 2006.

Las Cases, Emmanuel-Auguste-Dieudonné. *Mémorial de Sainte Hélène: Journal of the Private Life and Conversations of the Emperor Napoleon at Saint Helena*, Vol. IV. London: H. Colburn and co., 1823.

Leggiere, Michael V. *Blücher: Scourge of Napoleon*. Norman: University of Oklahoma Press, 2014.

Leggiere, Michael V. *Napoleon and the Struggle for Germany: The Franco-Prussian War of* 1813, *Volume* I: *The War of Liberation, Spring* 1813. Cambridge: Cambridge University Press, 2014.

Leggiere, Michael V. *Napoleon and the Struggle for Germany: The Franco-Prussian War of* 1813, *Volume* II: *The Defeat of Napoleon*. Cambridge: Cambridge University Press, 2015.

Leggiere, Michael V. *The Fall of Napoleon, Volume* I: *The Allied*

Invasion of France, 1813-1814. Cambridge: Cambridge University Press, 2007.

Le Moniteur Universel (May 22, 1799).

Louverture, Toussaint. "You want to slaughter all the whites?" on https://www.marxists.org/reference/archive/toussaint-louverture/1797/report.htm (accessed 28 August 2016).

Lyons, Martyn. "The Napoleonic Empire in Europe–Liberation or Exploitation?" in *Exploring the European Past: Texts & Images*, Second Edition, ed. Timothy E. Gregory. Mason: Cengage Learning, 2011. 10-11.

Macdonald, Jacques Étienne Joseph Alexandre, duc de Tarente. *Recollections of Marshal Macdonald, Duke of Tarentum*. Ed. Camille Rousset, tr. Stephen Louis Simeon. London: Richard Bentley and Son, 1892.

Markham, J. David. *Napoleon and Dr. Verling on St Helena*. Barnsley: Pen and Sword, 2005.

Markham, J. David. *The Road to St. Helena: Napoleon After Waterloo*. Barnsley: Pen and Sword, 2008.

Markham, Felix. *Napoleon*. New York: Penguin Books, 1966.

Martineau, Gilbert. *Madame Mère: Napoleon's Mother*. J. Murray, 1978.

Masson, Frederic. *Sex Life of an Emperor: The Many Loves of Napoleon Bonaparte*. Tucson: Fireship Press, 2009.

McErlean, J.M.P. "Le Blocus Continental: A Historical Revision," *First Empire: The International Magazine for the Napoleonic Enthusiast, Historian and Gamer* 94 (May/June 2007), 29.

McLynn, Frank. *Napoleon: A Biography*. New York: Skyhorse Publishing, Inc., 2011.

Muir, Rory. *Britain and the Defeat of Napoleon, 1807-1815*. New Haven and London: Yale University Press, 1996.

Muir, Rory. *Wellington: The Path to Victory, 1769-1814*. New Haven and London: Yale University Press, 2013.

Muir, Rory. *Wellington: Waterloo and the Fortunes of Peace, 1814-1852*. New Haven and London: Yale University Press, 2013.

Napoleon I, Emperor of the French. *Correspondance de Napoléon*

Ier; Publiée par ordre de l'empereur Napoléon III. Paris: Imprimerie Impériale, 1858-1869.

Napoleon I, Emperor of the French. *Letters and Documents of Napoleon, Volume I: The Rise to Power*, selected and translated by John Eldred Howard. London: The Cresset Press, 1961.

Popkin, Jeremy D. *A Concise History of the Haitian Revolution*. Chichester, West Sussex: Wiley-Blackwell, 2012.

Roberts, Andrew. *Napoleon, A Life*. New York: Penguin Group, 2014.

Rose, John Holland. *The Life of Napoleon I, Volume I*. New York: The MacMillan Company, 1902.

Rothenberg, Gunther E. *The Art of Warfare in the Age of Napoleon*. Bloomington and Indianapolis: Indiana University Press, 1980.

Sauvigny, Guillaume de Bertier de. *The Bourbon Restoration*. Tr. Lynn M. Case. Philadelphia: The University of Pennsylvania Press, 1966.

Shukoff, Peter. "Napoleon vs. Napoleon," *Epic Rap Battles of History*, https://www.youtube.com/watch?v=AeNYDwbm9qw (accessed June 2, 2016.)

Thomas, J. E. *Britain's Last Invasion: Fishguard 1797*. Tempus, 2007.

Thrasher, Peter Adam. *Pasquale Paoli: An Enlightened Hero, 1725-1807*. Hamden: Archon Books, 1970.

Tone, John Lawrence. *The Fatal Knot: The Guerrilla War in Navarre and the Defeat of Napoleon in Spain*. Chapel Hill and London: The University of North Carolina Press, 1994.

Tone, Theobald Wolfe. *The Writings of Theobald Wolfe Tone, 1763-98, Volume III: France, the Rhine, Lough Swilly and death of Tone, January 1797 to November 1798*, ed. T. W. Moody, R.B. McDowell and C. J. Woods. Oxford: Clarendon Press, 2007.

Tschudi, Clara. *Napoleon's Mother*. London: Swan Sonnenschein & Co., 1900.

Watson, Thomas Edward. *Napoleon: A Sketch of his Life, Character, Struggles and Achievements*. New York: The Macmillan Company, 1902.

Weider, Ben. "Napoleon and the Jews," *The Napoleon Series*, http://www.napoleon-series.org/ins/weider/c_jews.html (accessed September 25, 2016).

Zamoyski, Adam. 1812: *Napoleon's Fatal March on Moscow*. New York, HarperCollins, 2004.

Zarzeczny, Daniel. "Other Famous Napoleons," *History and Headlines*, http://www.historyandheadlines.com/other-famous-napoleons/ (accessed June 2, 2016).

Zarzeczny, Matthew. *Meteors that Enlighten the Earth: Napoleon and the Cult of Great Men*. Newcastle upon Tyne: Cambridge Scholars Publishing, 2012.

Zarzeczny, Matthew. "November 18, 1803: Winning Haitian Independence, but Without the Devil's Help!" on *History and Headlines*, http://www.historyandheadlines.com/winning-haitian-independence-without-devils-help/ (accessed January 3, 2017).

Suggested Reading

The number of articles and books written about Napoleon is breathtaking if not overwhelming. As such, it would be a task well beyond this volume to list or even discuss at too much length such a tremendous amount of scholarship of varying quality. Nevertheless, we can highlight some of the good starting places for further research beyond this brief introduction to one of history's most influential people. Although we do list several biographies of Napoleon here, they vary in length and perspective both in terms of nationality of the author and when they were published.

Abell, Lucia Elizabeth (Balcombe). *To Befriend an Emperor: Betsy Balcombe's Memoirs of Napoleon on St Helena.* Introduction by J. David Markham. Welwyn Garden City: Ravenhall Books, 2005. In the early days of Napoleon's exile on St Helena, Napoleon befriended a young lady named Betsy Balcombe. Years later she wrote her memoirs, which are some of the most interesting to come out of Napoleon's life. They show a personal side of Napoleon not often found in the literature.

Asprey, Robert. *The Reign of Napoleon Bonaparte.* New York: Basic Books, 2001. Asprey (1923–2009) was an American military historian and author who later in his life moved to Spain. He served in the U.S. Marines during World War II and the Korean War, receiving a Purple Heart and a Presidential Unit Citation for his service. He studied history throughout North America and Europe at the University of Iowa, Oxford University, the University of Vienna, and the University of Nice. This book on Napoleon, covering the period spanning from December 1805 to May 1821, came toward the end of Asprey's long career and has received praise from numerous reviewers from the *Boston Globe* and *History Magazine*, among others.

Austin, Paul Britten. *1812: Napoleon in Moscow.* London: Greenhill Books, 1995. Paul Britten Austin (1922–2005) worked as an

English author, translator, broadcaster, and administrator. He spent some 25 years working on his positively-reviewed trilogy about Napoleon's invasion of Russia, largely as told by those who participated in the invasion firsthand.

Blaufarb, Rafe. *Napoleon: Symbol for an Age: A Brief History with Documents*. Boston and New York: Bedford/St. Martin's, 2008. Part of The Bedford Series in History and Culture, an immensely valuable series for college and university professors, Blaufarb's contribution to numerous primary sources about Napoleon and life under his rule. This balanced account covers everything from politics to warfare. It is an excellent introduction to the various contemporary attitudes and opinions for and against Napoleon and his empire as organized by a top scholar of the era. Blaufarb earned his Ph.D. from the University of Michigan and currently is the Ben Weider Eminent Scholar Chair in Napoleonic History and, since 2006, the Director of the Institute on Napoleon and the French Revolution at Florida State University, a position previously held by Dr. Donald D. Horward, from 1998 until his retirement in 2005.

Blaufarb, Rafe and Claudia Liebeskind. *Napoleonic Foot Soldiers and Civilians: A Brief History with Documents*. Boston and New York: Bedford/St. Martin's, 2011. Blaufarb's second contribution to The Bedford Series in History and Culture includes additional concise excerpts from primary sources concerning the Napoleonic Era. This time, Blaufarb is joined by co-author Liebeskind, an associate professor of history at Florida State University. She earned her Ph.D. at the University of London.

Boudon, Jacques-Olivier. *Napoléon et les Cultes: Les religions en Europe àl'aube du XIXe siècle 1800-1815*. Paris: Librairie Arthème Fayard, 2002. Boudon (born 1962) is a French historian and professor at the University of Paris. Much of his work covers the Napoleonic Era and this particular book, for those of our readers who can read French, covers religion in Europe during Napoleon's reign as First Consul and then Emperor of the French.

Broers, Michael. *Europe Under Napoleon 1799-1815*. London and New York: Arnold, 1996. Broers, a lecturer in history at the

University of Leeds, emphasizes the experiences of those ruled by Napoleon rather than their ruler.

Chandler, David G. ***The Campaigns of Napoleon.*** **New York: Macmillan Publishing Company, Inc: 1966.** This large volume is the classic work on Napoleon's campaigns and battles. Chandler, one of the foremost Napoleonic scholars of his day, gives a level of detail that is amazing while also analyzing the effect of the various actions.

Chandler, David G. ***Dictionary of the Napoleonic Wars.*** **New York: Simon & Schuster, 1999.** More than a dictionary, this volume also contains dozens of maps, a chronological table, and bibliography.

Chandler, David G., ed. ***Napoleon's Marshals.*** **New York: Macmillan Publishing Company, 1987.** David G. Chandler (1934–2004) was a British historian, and former captain in Britain's army honored with multiple awards during his seventy years of life. This book covers the lives of twenty-six other celebrated military men who lived a century or so before Chandler. To cover the lives of the twenty-six men made Marshals of the French Empire by Napoleon, Chandler turned to some of the leading Napoleonic scholars of the late-twentieth centuries, some of whose names and works appear elsewhere on this annotated bibliography. This book is essential reading for learning about Napoleon's key subordinates.

Chandler, David G. ***The Military Maxims of Napoleon.*** **Cambridge, MA: Da Capo Press, 1995.** Chandler provides the book's introduction and commentary, but the bulk of the text are the words of Napoleon. Anyone looking for insights into how Napoleon waged war and thought war should be waged will find this book helpful.

Connelly, Owen. ***Napoleon's Satellite Kingdoms: Managing Conquered Peoples.*** **Malabar: Robert E. Krieger Publishing Company, 1990.** Connelly, an American historian who specialized in military history, was Distinguished Professor of History Emeritus at the University of South Carolina before passing away in 2011. As the book's title suggests, this book addresses the nature of Napoleon's rule over his various subject lands.

Conner, Susan P. ***The Age of Napoleon.*** **London: Greenwood Press,**

2004. This excellent and very readable book goes beyond dealing with just the traditional topics of Napoleonic history to explore the structure, society, daily life, and ultimate influence of Napoleonic France. Conner is an outstanding American historian, and this book gives an outstanding overview of all aspects of Napoleon and his times.

Cronin, Vincent. *Napoleon Bonaparte: An Intimate Biography.* New York: William Morrow & Company, 1972. Cronin was an influential British historian who wrote compelling biographies of several important historical figures. While he admittedly tends to take a positive view of Napoleon, he offers a wealth of detail in this very readable biography. A paperback version was released in 1995.

Ellis, Geoffrey. *Napoleon.* London: Longman, 1997. In this book, part of Longman's Profiles in Power series, Ellis tends to interpret Napoleon as both a realist and an opportunist, thereby taking a position in opposition to those presented by other contemporary scholars such as Martyn Lyons and Stuart Woolf.

Elting, John R. *Swords Around A Throne: Napoleon's Grande Armée.* New York: The Free Press, 1988. This book is essential reading for anyone wanting to know more about the nature and structure of Napoleon's military machine. Col. Elting presents a depth of knowledge untouched in any other book dealing with the subject. A paperback and Kindle version was released in 1997.

Erickson, Carolly. *Josephine: A Life of the Empress.* New York: St. Martin's Press, 1998. Erickson (born 1943) is an award-winning American author of historical fiction and non-fiction who lives in Hawaii. Her books tend to cover the lives of European history's most celebrated queens. Any exploration of Napoleon's life would be incomplete without also exploring the life of his greatest love and first wife whose name was perhaps the last name on his lips before his death.

Fain, Baron John. *Napoleon: How He Did It. The Memoirs of Baron Fain, First Secretary of the Emperor's Cabinet.* Forward by Jean Tulard. First English Edition of the Complete Original Manuscript [1829]. San Francisco: Proctor Jones Publishing Company, 1998.

As First Secretary of Napoleon's cabinet, Fain worked closely with Napoleon and those around him. His memoirs give fascinating insight into Napoleon's work habits and how and government operated.

Forshufvud, Sten and Ben Weider. ***Assassination at St. Helena: The Poisoning of Napoleon Bonaparte.*** **Forward by David Chandler. Vancouver: Mitchell Press, 1978.** This important book gives great detail of Napoleon's life on St Helena and lays out the case for the argument that Napoleon was poisoned.

Franceschi, Michel and Ben Weider. ***The Wars Against Napoleon: Debunking the Myth of the Napoleonic Wars.*** **New York: Savas Beatie LLC, 2008.** Franceschi began a military career in 1951 in France and eventually, by 1990, attained the rank of General of Corps. He co-authored this volume with world-renowned businessman and founder of the International Napoleonic Society Weider (1923–2008). The two authors clearly fall in the "for" Napoleon camp. Nevertheless, they do a sound job reminding readers that Napoleon hardly deserves the amount of blame he usually gets for starting and perpetuating the many wars in which he fought and/or led armies. Rather, his opponents were hardly paragons of peace.

Fregosi, Paul. ***Dreams of Empire: Napoleon and the First World War, 1792-1815.*** **New York: Carol Publishing Group, 1990.** Fregosi was a French-born and British-educated author who died in Brazil. This book is immensely helpful in getting a sense of the global scope of Napoleon's various wars and thus their importance well beyond Europe.

Geyl, Pieter. ***Napoleon, For and Against,*** **translated by Olive Renier. New Haven, CT; Yale University Press, 1948.** Geyl was a Dutch historian, who in 1940 wrote an article on how historians view Napoleon just before the German occupation during World War II. During the war, Geyl was eventually imprisoned for more than a year at Buchenwald concentration camp. Geyl's experiences with Hitler and Nazism during World War II clearly influenced his ideas of Napoleon and Bonapartism. *Napoleon, For and Against* provides an account of how French historians of different ages and views have regarded the French emperor as either a Corsican adventurer who brought death and destruction to France or as a patriotic Frenchman who brought glory and prosperity. Of course, the black and white "for and against" dichotomy is rather simplistic as one can reasonably have more moderate, less polarizing views of Napoleon. Nevertheless, in terms of an outstanding historiographic overview of French scholarship on Napoleon from Napoleon's actual lifetime to the early 1940s, you can do no worse that Geyl's classic.

Grab, Alexander. *Napoleon and the Transformation of Europe.* New York: Palgrave Macmillan, 2003. This outstanding scholar looks at how Napoleon worked not only to rule France but also to establish French dominance over all of Europe. In so doing he argues that Napoleon was as much European as he was French.

Guerrini, Maurice. *Napoleon and Paris: Thirty Years of History.* New York: Walker and Company, 1970. Guerrini's contribution to our understanding of Napoleon concerns the numerous realized and planned building projects undertaken and imagined by Napoleon for his capital city. The book includes maps that help readers to envision how Napoleon imagined Paris would look had he ultimately triumphed.

Haythornthwaite, Philip J. *The Napoleonic Sourcebook.* London: Arms and Armour, 1996. This book is a handy encyclopedia of the campaigns, weapons, nations, people, and more associated with the Napoleonic Wars. It contains many key terms, maps, illustrations, and charts to help provide readers with a ready reference guide to the era.

Holtman, Robert B. *The Napoleonic Revolution.* Baton Rouge and London: Louisiana State University Press, 1967. Holtman, a Ph.D. recipient from the University of Wisconsin and then a professor of history at Louisiana State University, presents Napoleon as "a revolutionary innovator whose influence touched nearly every aspect of European political and social life and has extended even to our own times," according to the book's back cover. More specifically, Holtman identifies Napoleon's revolutionary innovations with regards to the military, law, economics, relations with the Catholic Church, education, propaganda, and nationalism. To that end, this book is helpful in understanding Napoleon's lasting importance for Europe and how his reign can be considered a revolution in its own right following the French Revolution of 1789 to 1799.

Kafker, Frank A. and James A. Laux. *Napoleon and His Times: Selected Interpretations.* Malabar, FL: Robert E. Krieger, 1989. The debate begun in Geyl's *Napoleon, For and Against* arguably continues in this no longer up-to-date collection of various opinions by leading experts of the Napoleonic Age. For anyone wanting a historiographic overview of the essential interpretations of Napoleon and his times, he or she should first read Geyl's study and then this one as a sort of unofficial sequel.

Kagan, Frederick W. *Napoleon and Europe: The End of the Old Order,* 1801-1805. Cambridge: The Perseus Books Group, 2006. Kagan (born 1970) is a former professor of military history at the U.S. Military Academy at West Point and a current resident scholar at the American Enterprise Institute. He hails from a distinguished family of notable historians that includes his father, brother, and wife. At 774 pages, *The End of the Old Order* is a fairly detailed account of events taking place over just a few years that nevertheless transformed Europe. Kagan made use of Austrian, German, French, and Russian archival sources for this extensive study on European political, diplomatic, and military history.

Lyons, Martyn. *Napoleon Bonaparte and the Legacy of the French Revolution.* Basingstoke, UK: Palgrave Macmillan, 1994. Lyons produced his study of both France and the Napoleonic Empire with a student audience in mind.

Marchand, Louis-Joseph. *In Napoleon's Shadow. Being the First English Language Edition of the complete Memoirs of Louis-Joseph Marchand, Valet and Friend of The Emperor* 1811-1821. Produced by Proctor Jones. Original notes of Jean Bourguignon and Henry Lachouque. Preface by Jean Tulard. San Francisco: Proctor Jones Publishing Company, 1998. Marchand was one of Napoleon's most trusted subordinates whom he considered a friend. Unlike some memoirs, Marchand's are straightforward and not self-serving. He writes in a simple and very readable manner, giving us unique insight into the everyday life of Napoleon.

Markham, Felix. *Napoleon*. New York: Penguin Books, 1966. Markham's biography of Napoleon was the first book-length biography of Napoleon that Dr. Zarzeczny read in his relative youth and thus deserves a good deal of credit for further sparking Zarzeczny's continued fascination with the French emperor. What stood out perhaps most was toward the end of the book when Markham quotes Napoleon's vision of a unified Europe, a topic that eventually became the focus of Zarzeczny's thesis for his Master's degree at Kent State University.

Markham, J. David. *The Road to St. Helena: Napoleon After Waterloo*. Barnsley: Pen and Sword, 2008. Much has been written about various phases and periods of Napoleon's life. Oddly, relatively little has been written about the period between Waterloo and Napoleon's exile on St Helena. Yet that period offers great insight into both Napoleon and France during that critical period. Markham vividly describes the very complex political situation in France as the Allies were moving on Paris and various factions in French politics were vying for power. Napoleon's trip from Paris to Malmaison and ultimately to destiny is fascinating material, and Markham, using many excellent sources, tells the story well.

Markham, J. David. *Napoleon for Dummies*. Hoboken: Wiley Publishing, Inc., 2005. Markham presents an organized overview of Napoleon and his times in a way that is accessible to anyone looking to learn the essential information about one of history's key figures. The book serves as a great study guide.

Markham, J. David. *Napoleon's Road to Glory: Triumphs, Defeats & Immortality*. London: Brassey's, 2003. Markham's biography of Napoleon is among the better post-millennium accounts of Napoleon's life that goes into greater detail than the biography you are currently reading.

McLynn, Frank. *Napoleon, A Biography*. New York: Arcade Publishing, 2002. McLynn (born 1941) is a critically acclaimed British author, biographer, historian, and journalist educated at Wadham College, Oxford and the University of London. Among the praise heaped upon this particular biography, *Publisher's Weekly* describes this 739-page book as "one of the best of the new breed" and as "a well-researched, convincing portrait."

Nafziger, George F. *Historical Dictionary of the Napoleonic Era.* Lanham and London: The Scarecrow Press, Inc., 2002. Part of a series titled *Ancient Civilizations and the Historical Eras*, at 353 pages, this dictionary is a shorter alternative to the 570 pages found in Chandler's longer dictionary listed above. Nafziger (born 1949) is a prolific American writer and editor of numerous books and articles in military history (including many on the Napoleonic Wars) who also served in the U.S. Navy during the Vietnam War. In any case, it is interesting to get a British perspective on the same era in Chandler's dictionary and an American perspective in Nafziger's dictionary.

North, Jonathan, ed. *The Napoleon Options: Alternate Decisions of the Napoleonic Wars.* London: Greenhill Books, 2000. This edited volume contains ten counterfactuals of the Napoleonic Wars and thus indicates how important decision-making is for military leaders while also giving readers entertaining explorations into what might have been. Each counterfactual is written by a different well-known Napoleonic author.

Prendergast, Christopher. *Napoleon and History Painting: Antoine-Jean Gros's La Bataille d'Eylau.* Oxford: Clarendon Press, 1997. Prendergast, a Professor of Modern French Literature and Fellow of King's College, Cambridge, argues, according to the book's back cover, "that under Napoleon, French history painting, especially battle painting, encountered a series of questions as to its nature and function. These questions arose in part from the (often contradictory) demands of a propaganda-machine operating within a post-revolutionary crisis of political legitimation, but also from changes in artistic taste which both retained and re-directed an earlier notion of the civic responsibilities of the history painter." Thus, this book is helpful for readers interested in a scholarly exploration of Napoleonic art.

Rose, John Holland. *The Life of Napoleon I.* New York: The MacMillan Company, 1902. Rose (1855–1942), an English historian, was educated at Bedford Modern School, at Owen's College, Manchester, and at Christ's College, Cambridge. His two-volume life of Napoleon is probably Rose's most famous and influential work.

Woloch, Isser. *Napoleon and his Collaborators: The Making of a Dictatorship.* New York and London: W. W. Norton & Company, 2001. Woloch is an award-winning Professor of History at Columbia University. His book explores not only the rise of Napoleon but also "the dilemmas of collaboration with dictatorial power."

Woolf, Stuart. *Napoleon's Integration of Europe.* London and New York: Routledge, 1991. Woolf's book is a must-read for anyone trying to draw comparisons between Napoleon's Grand Empire over two hundred years ago and the European Union today.

Zarzeczny, Matthew D. *Meteors that Enlighten the Earth: Napoleon and the Cult of Great Men.* Newcastle upon Tyne: Cambridge Scholars Publishing, 2012. The best overview available on what historical figures were admired by Napoleon at various times in his life and why. Also, an excellent source on understanding "hero worship" in general and how it motivates us for good or ill.

We must reiterate that the preceding list is only a starting place for delving deeper into the life and times of Napoleon Bonaparte. The above represents some of our favorites, but again there are many, many more books out there worthy of consideration. Our list of sources found elsewhere in this volume expands upon the above suggestions for further reading and among the entries found on that list that are not elaborated upon above, our esteemed colleague and friend Alexander Mikaberidze of Louisiana State University in Shreveport recommends the following books in particular: the new Napoleon biographies by Phillip Dwyer, Alan Forrest, and Patrice Gueniffrey; Katherine Aalestad's new work on the Continental System, Charles Esdaile's recent books on the Peninsular War, Michael Leggiere's great works on the 1813-1814 Campaigns (as well as his biography of Field Marshal Blücher); Rory Muir's excellent studies on Britain's involvement in the Napoleonic War, including his magisterial two-volume biography of Arthur Wellesley, 1st Duke of Wellington; and the new *Correspondance générale* (Napoleon's correspondence) that is superior to the much older versions.

About the Authors

J. David Markham is an internationally recognized scholar and writer and the president of the International Napoleonic Society. He has written, edited and/or contributed to ten books on Napoleon, including *Napoleon for Dummies* and *The Road to St Helena: Napoleon after Waterloo*. He has appeared in television documentaries, lectured at conferences and museums around the world, and co-created with Cameron Reilly, the popular "Napoleon 101" podcast. In 2014, he was appointed a Knight in the Order of the French Academic Palms, France's highest civilian-only award. He has also been awarded the INS Legion of Merit and the Napoleonic Historical Society Colonel John H. Etling Scholar Award, the highest academic recognition for the two groups.

A Fellow of the International Napoleonic Society and an adjunct instructor at Ashland University and Kent State University at Stark, in addition to John Carroll University, **Matthew D. Zarzeczny** has written widely on Napoleon Bonaparte. He is the author of *Meteors That Enlighten the Earth: Napoleon and the Cult of Great Men* and the founder of the popular website www.historyandheadlines.com.

A Word from the Publisher

Thank you for reading *Simply Napoleon*!

If you enjoyed reading it, we would be grateful if you could help others discover and enjoy it too.

Please review it with your favorite book provider such as Amazon, BN, Kobo, Apple Books, or Goodreads, among others.

Again, thank you for your support and we look forward to offering you more great reads.

CPSIA information can be obtained
at www.ICGtesting.com
Printed in the USA
LVHW041733091220
673728LV00004B/673

9 781943 657193